# The Lane via Benghazi

The tale of a smile and an open hand

Denis T Logan

iUniverse, Inc.
Bloomington

# The Lane via Benghazi

*Copyright © 2011 by Denis T Logan*

*All rights reserved. No part of this book may be used or reproduced by any means, graphic, electronic, or mechanical, including photocopying, recording, taping or by any information storage retrieval system without the written permission of the publisher except in the case of brief quotations embodied in critical articles and reviews.*

*The views expressed in this work are solely those of the author and do not necessarily reflect the views of the publisher, and the publisher hereby disclaims any responsibility for them.*

*iUniverse books may be ordered through booksellers or by contacting:*

*iUniverse*
*1663 Liberty Drive*
*Bloomington, IN 47403*
*www.iuniverse.com*
*1-800-Authors (1-800-288-4677)*

*Because of the dynamic nature of the Internet, any web addresses or links contained in this book may have changed since publication and may no longer be valid.*

*Any people depicted in stock imagery provided by Thinkstock are models, and such images are being used for illustrative purposes only.*

*Certain stock imagery © Thinkstock.*

*ISBN: 978-1-4620-0526-0 (sc)*
*ISBN: 978-1-4620-0527-7 (ebk)*

*Printed in the United States of America*

*iUniverse rev. date: 5/11/2011*

*For my dear mum, my wife Carole and our two sons, Den and Chris. Now at last the story is in print, you won't have to spend the rest of your lives listening to it.*

# Contents

CHAPTER 1: The Lake District . . . . . . . . . . . . . . . . . 1

CHAPTER 2: The thin dotted line . . . . . . . . . . . . . . 22

CHAPTER 3: Excuse me, which way is Tunisia? . . . . 38

CHAPTER 4: Egg shells . . . . . . . . . . . . . . . . . . . . . . 60

CHAPTER 5: Lovely day for a swim . . . . . . . . . . . . . 75

CHAPTER 6: On top of my world . . . . . . . . . . . . . 115

CHAPTER 7: Six feet three and full of muscle . . . . 137

CHAPTER 8: No paperwork, bogged down anyway 146

CHAPTER 9: The meaning of green . . . . . . . . . . . . 154

CHAPTER 10: Backwards to Christmas . . . . . . . . . 159

CHAPTER 11: Breaking bread . . . . . . . . . . . . . . . . 171

CHAPTER 12: All gone, job done . . . . . . . . . . . . . 191

# CHAPTER 1:

## The Lake District

I was born Denis Timothy Logan, but people call me Den. I prefer it that way. More personal, no airs and graces. Just Den. That way we know where we stand: you and me. The journey started in a cathedral town, St Albans, Hertfordshire, England, mercifully left unscarred by bombs falling from the sky of the second World War. The eldest of four, with two brothers and a little sister. Being born in a cathedral town, with all that history and old buildings and the grandeur of the cathedral itself and the extensive lawns and the lakes, and a Bishop, well, it sounds impressive. But 6 Blacksmiths Lane was another world far removed from choirs, surplices, fat candles and high church. I was a nervous lad, always on edge, doing whatever I could to smile and be helpful. A tense smile. Right from an early age, on edge, anxious. A spontaneous and hefty slap around the lug-hole for burping does that to you. A labourer's heavy heavy hand. Wait for it. Stomach tenses up. Anticipation. Ouch! No, no choirs at 6 Blacksmiths Lane. My dad was rough, violent, unpredictable even when we knew what was about to happen. The other five citizens of his burly empire tip-toed around him, and me somehow like a boxer caught within the four ropes and four corner posts of four walls of a two-up and two-down cottage. In the ring, you can't hide.

By the time the war was over, I was old enough to know it was over. Gone were the days when I would be sent out by mum to the baker's shop across the road to buy a loaf. When I got back home with it, smelling oven-fresh and beautifully warm in my hands, mum would take it and break it in half and pull out a handful of dough, roll it into a ball and then carefully erase the ticks in the ration book that indicated we had received our portion of government issue sugar or tea. Dough didn't scuff up the paper the way an eraser did. It was the only way she could feed us. Dad drank. I remember the rent was six shillings a week. Dad drank, twelve pints a night, which cost more than the rent and the food combined. So my mother had to cheat, while teaching us to be honest. Life's a paradox whichever way you look at it. The bombs had long since left their craters in the country, but the blows kept falling at 6 Blacksmiths Lane, and couldn't be avoided. Not by me. My brothers and my sister were spared: I was the eldest, and therefore first in line, and took the hits, and not trying to be noble and protect the others either; I just couldn't get out of the way often enough.

My first bike was a two-wheeler Fairy cycle, a relic going on forty years old, with direct spoke wheels and solid tyres that were always coming off the rim. I used to ride it around the lakes, those two lakes that were my place. One day a tyre came off and there happened to be a small escorted column of prisoners of war coming past me, maybe going to work in the cathedral grounds or to dig graves, but to the kid I was they were just convenient passersby. I picked one out at random. "Scuse me, mister. I can't do this myself." I probably made the question out of gestures and an open asking smile. The man I chose wore a woollen khaki cap, and a dark greatcoat. He gave me a smile, came across. He spoke in a language. With his big hands he readily set the tyre back where it was supposed to be, tapped me on the head and trotted off to catch up with the column. It was such a different feeling, that tap on the head, from others I had received, and this from a prisoner of war. Everywhere paradoxes. I sat on the bike and watched as they wound their way around my lakes and up towards the cathedral. Content to be mobile again, I continued with my exploration of the safety zone I had cordoned off in the unpredictable world, my territory, my place, free as a bird. I looked up the hill. They had gone.

That country was my refuge the lake, actually two lakes, the large one and the small one, connected by a brick footbridge, with *The Fighting Cocks* at the holy end of the world and, in another country, Blacksmiths Lane at the other. It was best being out of doors, and the lake was my place. I practically lived there and knew it the way a painter knows the brush strokes of a painting. It was my place, my world, so absolutely different from the world inside 6 Blacksmiths Lane only a stone's throw away. I loved it. I still love it. Going back there would be like going back to my first real home: water, ducks, trees, places to hide, places to run, grass. My world between the cathedral and home, and no need to escape. It must be hard living as a prisoner of war.

I'd play there with my mates, Bomber Lewis, Dave and Barry, climbing trees, watching birds nesting in buckets or old tins, robins, and the wrens with their nest like a green ball with a hole in it. Why the blackbirds and thrushes were so careless as to make their eggs so easy to find I couldn't figure. There was something charming about seeing eggs in the apparent warmth and safety of a nest and the eggs so fragile. I was near enough on speaking terms with any number of fir trees and old yews. Other than that, happiness was finding a stick and poking around the woods not far from our flint-stone school.

The Lake introduced me to swimming. The water is about fifteen centimetres deep on one side and going down to a depth of maybe a metre at the other. My mum had knitted me a pair of black woollen trunks. I was proud of them, all brand new as they were, and I felt posh as well, as good as at the sea-side, ready to swim the Channel. I flexed what muscles I had, slapped my face a couple of times, picked up courage, took a deep breath, jumped in the deep end and went straight to the bottom. I waded around in up to my shins in mud and slime, feeling for bottles with my toes, and pressing duck shit into the mud and feeling small fish against my legs. I then waded out of the mire. Wool is efficiently water-absorbent. The weight of the water pulled my brand new trunks down, so that it looked as if I had two dead ferrets strapped to my waist and a gargoyle between my legs. I was not feeling quite so posh.

Another thing mum did for me was to introduce me to the mystique of flying. Perhaps my sixth birthday present was a gift few boys have received, but secretly most boys my age at the time would dream of having. It was a genuine leather aviator's flying-cap which she had probably found at a Surplus store and at a cost within her budget. The cap may well have been unused - the War had only come to an end two years before. At the time most kids dreamed of flying and pilots had a mystique about them because so few people had flown. Recently the same mystique cloaks astronauts, but astronauts do not have the same mystique as the first pilots did. Often the pilot flew solo, just the man, the machine, the stars, the storms, and, at the time, the enemy, and hoping to get back to the rest of the squadron. Of course it was slightly too big for me, but that didn't matter - the child's imagination over-rides those details: it was authentic, the real thing, and no other kid at school had one. It was also perfect for winter, being snug and, being lined leather, very warm. The padded ear sections had a zip across them which the pilot would undo when flying with headphones on. Further adding to its value to me as a child was that it was not like a skull cap, but had a fitted section at the back that was shaped to cover the very tops of the shoulders around the neck. When the pilot had his flying jacket on, the jacket fitted over the top of the shoulder section of the cap and that added insulation. But the value of the insulation to me was not in keeping the air out. I wore it to school. We used to get snow in winter and, as kids do, one of the really fun things to do was to stuff snow down the back of someone's neck. They couldn't do that with me, and that felt good. The bullies left me alone.

Towards my last year at school swapping things had become the rage, the easiest way of acquiring stuff without having to pay cash. I liked playing mouth-organ and in exchange for a catapult I acquired this lovely Hohner model, with the lever on one side, to change key. That lasted a while and then guns nudged the mouth-organ out, swapping it as I did for a 4.10 Spanish shotgun, fascinating because it folded up to fit into a poacher's pocket. Before long I had quite a small armoury: dueling pistols, snub-nosed 45 revolver, lady pistols, Verey pistols, several .22 air rifles, and, prize possession, a Winchester 75 two-band rifle – me and John Wayne at High Noon. Me and my mates would go out into the wild west woods of St Albans as cowboys, or make-believe hoodlums or whatever and give the bad guys what was coming to them. Handling a Spanish folding 4.10 double-barreled shotgun felt like what I imagined holding an expensive wine glass might feel. And for me there was a fascination in the mechanics, the tooling, the construction, the materials and the feel to the hand and the smell of the wood and the oil and the cordite. It is a strange image for a small cathedral city, but one day I came to have an elephant gun, in St Albans, where elephants are as common as a circus coming to town. And yes, there was the temptation to go out and see what kind of damage it might do to a mature oak tree, but no, I never did that, officer, it wasn't me.

But there was one encounter with an officer of the law, Sergeant Goodge. I was out walking with dad through the woods alongside which ran the main road going north out of town. Must have been wintertime because the trees were bare. Dad had his hunting rifle with him – in those days it was not uncommon for people to have hunting rifles, as long as they had a license. He spotted two pigeons high up in a tree. He set the rifle against his shoulder, took careful aim, and fired. The two pigeons tumbled clattering through the branches, followed by feathers floating here and there. We carried on our merry way. As luck would have it Sergeant Goodge, on duty in his bobby's uniform, happened to be wheeling his bike through the woods as well. He must have heard the gun's report. In a leisurely fashion he called out to dad, "Do you have a license for that, sir?" Dad called back that of course he does, and showed it to the Sergeant once he had stopped beside us, bike propped against his hip. Everything was in order, but he did make a note of dad's name and address. Two days later a summons arrived in the mail, giving notice that an offence had been committed, namely discharging a firearm within fifty metres of a main thoroughfare.

As far as school goes, I was not so good at school. Too edgy, too afraid to ask questions of the teachers when I had not understood. I just let the questions slide and slipped further and further behind with those unasked questions, failing particularly well at maths, almost with honours. Though I fell short of being a trouble-maker, my energies did often find their outlet in mischief, pranks, and taking it to the bullies. In other words I stood my ground and might have spent more energy standing my ground than studying. On the other hand, I did walk away with some of those highly valued pieces of paper, after my time at Townsend C. of E. Boys' Secondary Modern 'university' of the lower classes and the downwardly mobile: Metalwork (practical and theory), and English Literature. Makes me laugh. What an innovative combination, Logan. Metalwork and English Literature. You'll go far. Equally on the positive side, and for four years in a row, I was Number One at gymnastics. My childhood experiences had taught me the value of being quick-footed, nimble, agile, flexible, keeping strong, but not aggressive - boxing I could live without; it was too familiar, and the last thing I wanted to do was to hurt someone else. So there I would be at the peak of my scholastic learning curve: certified as competent in Metalwork and English Literature and excellent in gymnastics. Hardly enough to qualify me for the Foreign Office or further adventures at Yale. But the enjoyment of gymnastics also had another pay-off: a spring in my step when dancing, in my teenage years and beyond, at the local dance halls. I had a good sense of rhythm; it was a natural progression to bopping and grooving after all that bobbing and weaving and ducking for cover, using the ropes as an ally, leaning left and right, swaying back over the kitchen table, and maybe getting away with a lighter blow than would have happened just standing there and taking it.

As familiar as the drunken mayhem were the meals. Pig's trotters and cabbage. We were hungry. The food was hot. It tasted good, really good. And sheep's head stew. What a delicacy! The head would be too big to fit into the largest pot my mum had, meaning that the open jaw of the head would be sticking out between the lid and the rim of the heavily used pot, its teeth bared as if it was ready to eat us. But we didn't see anything gruesome or scary about that image: it was normal and it was food and it was hot. We ate everything, brains and all, licked our lips and asked for more.

One very vivid scene comes alive in my head a lifetime later. It is wintertime and the snow does not lay crisp and even: there isn't any. It's cold, even inside the house. My brothers and sister are asleep, clutching the house bricks warmed in the oven and wrapped in old newspaper - our hot water bottles. My mum, Bridget, and my dad are arguing, about money, the lack of money, where's the bloody money, I know you've got the money hidden somewhere, woman, do I have to use this to get it out a you .... I am at the upstairs window, looking through the curtains. I see mum, in her nightie, barefoot, being chased down the terraced house lane in the middle of the night, by dad slashing away behind her with a carving knife. I watched them disappear, got into bed and stared at the ceiling, and fell asleep. She must have escaped somehow because she was there again at breakfast time, as if nothing had happened. How she ever plucked up courage to creep back in the house is beyond me, but I never mentioned what I had seen. Despite all that, she never broke faith with dad, until we had all as good as grown up, physically. Then she met a man who actually treated her like a real woman, and, enough being enough, she made a long postponed decision and at last got something of what she deserved. You may not want to fight, but caught in a war what do you do? She had done what she had to, and consequently we all survived both wars.

Being Irish, dad wore a Donegal suit, tweed, good condition, not quite Saville Row, but respectable. He was a navvy, but off duty (down the pub) he was dapper; collar and tie, black wavy hair full of Brylcreem. He would poke his head around the kitchen door and say, "Tatta for a while" and he'd be gone, down the pub. We'd hear the front door slam, breathe a sigh, and sit and listen to Dick Barton on the valve radio. I used to go and get the battery recharged every week. That was a pleasant walk along Folly Lane to Darby's Electricals. The battery was a clear glass container, not so heavy, and with a metal carrying handle. The practical things appealed to me, and I enjoyed seeing things work properly the way they should. That gave me pleasure, perhaps the pleasure of a sense of at least having some element of control in my universe that was so wildly out of control. Dad never once used my given name, Den. To him I was 'mate', not worth a name really. Or perhaps it was an attempt to establish a bond, like between mates. Benefit of the doubt.

By fourteen I had duodenal ulcers. All the stress, the tension, sometimes the fear of paying the ultimate price in this war of inexplicable violence. Cause and effect, and not by choice. I was once so eaten out by pain I believed I was going to die. It was at school, and the pain seized hold of my innards and squeezed until I couldn't stand it. I rushed out of the classroom, past Mr. Miles, desperate. My mum worked at Woolworths in the centre of the town. I went there, almost crawled there. Where else do you go as a kid if you are in such pain that only death is going to take it away. I found her. She got me to the hospital. I have been on medication ever since. But I have been fortunate, still able-bodied, full of energy, and swim these days in a nice little above-ground pool in the back garden, neck-deep in clean filtered water, with neighbours and friends, summer sunshine, and a glass of beer or wine to be thankful for. And a willing smile. "Fancy another one?" "Don't mind if I do. Cheers, Den."

My dad was a navvy. I never saw him working at his job. I of course can still remember his face - I never forget a face - but I never saw his face sweating as he laboured. Some 60 years after leaving Blacksmiths Lane, I found myself back in St Albans, visiting relatives. I am walking along the street with my wife, Carole. Ahead of us a head moves up and down just above a hole in the pavement as the body works a pick axe. The head is wearing a flat cap. As we pass him, I glance down, see a 60 plus something face, and pieces click into place. A few metres further along I say to my wife. "Wait here, Carole. I have to go back to that guy. I am sure I know him." "How can you know him? We haven't lived here for heaven knows how long." I go back anyway and say hello. He stops working, moves the flat cap from his head, and wipes the sweat away with the back of the same hand. "Sorry to interrupt you, but are you John Bartlett? Three sisters? Went to St Michaels, the flint school? Yes?" He looks completely dazed. "Yes. I am. How did you know?" "I'm Denis Logan …." "Ah, yes, so you are ...." and he climbs out of the hole, cleans his hands off on some lint in his pocket and gives my outstretched hand a firm shake. "Denis Logan. Fancy that. You had a brother Tommy and, I think, let me see, a sister called Annette. Well, I'll be buggered. That was in 1947! How on earth did you remember me?" "Your face, John. Your face. I never forget a face." I felt satisfied as Carole and I walked on. I looked back and saw John staring after us. Yes, I told myself, I feel satisfied. It was as if I had met my dad for the first time in a state of peace.

By the time my year withdrew from the educational system, compulsory service in the armed forces was no longer required. So I got a job. Tea-boy and Junior Clerk for Thompson & Debenhams, Solicitors. I suppose, compared with home, the offices were well-appointed, a tad on the solemn side, subdued with respect but always peaceful too. That was good. A respite. I did the post, taking it to the post office, and taking mail marked "By Hand" to addresses near by. It was good to be out in the open air.

Overall, though, the job was morbid. Dull offices, dark-stained oak, polished floors and the smell of wax, a lot of silence, and codicils, affidavits, old women and death. From the main offices upstairs a constant movement of pipe and cigarette smoke drifted through the still atmosphere. Somewhere to mark time but when I needed a breath of fresh air I made delivery of some more letters marked "By Hand", whenever I could. One day the delivery route took me near the market place right at the heart of the town, close to the Clock Tower that everyone knew had been there for eight or nine hundred years. I was already feeling old. It was Friday. I saw an old schoolmate of mine outside Halfords, putting rucksacks and other stuff on display outside. I went up to him, with some undelivered envelopes still in my hand.

"Hey, Derek. What's it like working here at Halfords. I need a change. In fact, is there a job here?"

He thought there could be. I went inside and asked for the manager. He had some questions. How old are you? Where do you live? Did you finish school? The usual line of intense questioning required to secure a job for life. Probing questions, such as, "Do you have a bicycle?" I said I did. "Well," he said, "you can start Monday." It wasn't the Foreign Office, but the money was better than the solicitor was paying me to make tea, make clients feel at home, and make mail go here and there. I went back through the heavy oak door of Thompson and Debenhams, and announced that I was going to start at Halfords next Monday. "Thanks for letting me know, Mr. Logan. I had the feeling you wouldn't be staying long. All the best." No gold watch for me perhaps, but I did get a first class personal reference, the first of my working life, and I still have it, in the original envelope.

No one was behind me as a kid. No one to say, "You can do that, boy, you can do that." That's what made life very hard. It wasn't so much the kicks, and the punches and the slaps across the face or the dread or the ulcers no one should have at that young age. It was having no one behind me. It wasn't the teachers or the war or stuff like that. Just no one to say, "You can do that, boy, you can do that. Go for it. I'm right behind you if you fall." I did not know what I was looking for but something in me knew that I had to be that 'other' behind me, and just tell myself, "You can do that, boy, you can do that. Go for it."

But go for what? All I knew was that what was around me was not what I needed or deserved, and I did not want to accept a slow death as so many of my school mates had done, to surrender even before the battle had actually started in earnest. Finish school, find some kind of job, meet a girl, get married before or after she gets pregnant, keep working, wait, stay active, read the newspapers, a bit on the side. No, not for me, and not for Derek either. We became our own support network, though we never thought of it like that: we both needed a dose of life that was out there somewhere, and no compulsory time in the armed forces to reveal it for us.

The change from Thompson and Debenhams to Halfords was probably the most significant of my entire life, as far as having a job is concerned. From all those lifeless documents secreted in sealed envelopes, the dark stained panelling, manning the six-line phone exchange, "Hello, Good afternoon, sir, Thompson and Debenhams. May I help you?.... Hold on please, sir, I will go and ask...." From white sheets of paper and the merciless black bakelite telephone receiver back in its cradle, from that to jumping into the role of Junior Clerk handling bike spares, motor parts, tins of stuff to repair other stuff like cracked engine blocks, clutch and brake cables, sealants, tins of touch-up paint, stocklists, sales, colours everywhere, change, cash in the till, movement, people to talk to, learning that selling is not pushing but guiding customers to identify what they want and letting them make the decision and telling them that that is what I would have done if I was in their shoes, and mean it. "Congratulations. Given the budget, I'd say you've made a good choice. Any problems, just let me know. Name's Den." And a smile and an open hand. It was exciting. I was involved. I enjoyed the smells, and remembered my first bike. This was me. I enjoyed the customers, even the difficult ones: I was learning from all of them.

After a few years a new store opened in a neighbouring town, Hemel Hempstead. Two levels. Upstairs, car and motorcycle spare parts, with cycles and camping equipment downstairs. I was nearly twenty and owned my first machine, prouder than I'd felt in my unsoiled woollen swimming trunks. It was an Italian job, a Moto-Rumi scooter, 125 cc twin exhaust. What a joy going to and from work! and never mind the weather, there would be no more sweating on a bicycle for me. In today's language, you could say I felt funky. The store was moving into self-service, which was all the trend, towards what is called efficiency. I didn't mind: I had my Moto-Rumi and could go anywhere. I was on the move.

Derek had become a close friend and I now called him Degs. We talked, did the pubs now and again, and talked, about the future. Young men do that. What were the options? Trudge on. Girl. Marriage. Baby. Another baby. Pushchairs. A second hand car. Go for a council house. Get entrenched, and, just when you don't want it, get retrenched as well, default on the mortgage.... "Is that what you want, Degs?" "No, Den, we can do better than that, surely." We pondered a lot. The world's a big place and must be somewhere beyond St Albans and Hemel. But what to do? with no one behind you?

When you can't find the limits, throw your net as wide and as far and as high and handsome as you can. I pondered. What's furthest from Hemel? And I threw my net high and wide and far and caught .… New Zealand! Yes! That's it! There's nothing further away than New Zealand. We'll go for broke.

One day, I float the idea, casual as you like. "I'm going to New Zealand. I've never been abroad." "New Zealand! How?" And it went from there, after bouts of bravado laughter, that adrenalin of the wild idea flirted with. But we kept talking about it. We started asking questions, like how would you actually get to New Zealand? In those days, you could go through the system, and apply for an assisted passage to the colony, pay your £10, get on a boat, and arrive wherever immigrant boats arrived. But that didn't appeal. We wanted to make the journey our discovery of the world, at our own pace, work our way, down through France, Spain, ferry from Gibraltar, tour around North Africa where Rommel and Montgomery had been not long before but for other purposes, and then meander around the middle east, Nasser, the pyramids, Cyprus, somehow get to Sarawak, and then the boat or boats down to the right a bit towards New Zealand. And then see what happened. Mad. We laughed. But we kept it to ourselves, and kept working on the idea. "Den, I reckon we should do it. What have we got to lose?" "Well, maybe you're right: it's now or never, Derek. The longer we leave it the harder it will get."

I knew North Africa was some distance south of where St Albans and the dormitory towns were. That's really all I knew. Standing behind the counter at Halfords, I closed my eyes and imagined. Mud huts, unimaginable heat, scorpions, men wearing the red fez, crossing the Straits of Gibraltar, the other side of which would see the water immediately give way to a brown expanse of nothing. No trees. Nowhere to shelter. Just a brown expanse of sand for ever and our tyre marks all the way to ….

At that time, the Murphy Radio factory in Welwyn Garden City, another nearby dormitory town for the London overspill, had vacancies for people to do the soldering on electronic circuit boards - a natural progression from going to get batteries charged for the old radio. Being technical work the pay was better, some £2 a week extra, which was significant at a time when £1000 a year was very good money indeed and an income all of us dreamed of earning. We changed jobs, but we didn't change our plan, which had started to take on a life of its own, and had become irresistible. We needed the extra money and the training in electronics would serve us well anyway, perhaps, one day. Times were changing and life was picking up speed.

Somehow the idea became a decision. Derek had a car. We'd go in that. It was a Ford Prefect, two door saloon, side valve engine, 1172 cc, three gears, vacuum operated windscreen wipers that stopped if you had to press down hard on the accelerator, and in good working order, on English roads at least. We started buying things we'd need. A two-man Bukta tent, a single ring Gaz burner for cooking on, two tin plates and a couple of tin mugs. A fully equipped expedition to the antipodes! We thought of sponsorship and wrote to Ovaltine, who in fact supplied a couple of cartons of biscuits, for health and energy. We remarked to each other how appropriate it was that the car should be a light beige colour, kind of colour co-ordinated with the sand of the Sahara we planned to cross. It did not occur to us that such livery would be the perfect camouflage in the desert. (We learned later how hard it is to find a beige Ford Prefect in the sands of the Sahara. That's how green we were. No idea!) We made inquiries - passports, visas and stuff like that - and it was all hit and miss really since we didn't know anyone who had been abroad except a couple of school friends who had joined the army to discover the world, and they were out there somewhere, wherever the world was. Injections! The local doctor pumped us up with injections for yellow fever, small pox and cholera, but the only place you could get an injection for malaria was at the B.O.A.C. terminal in London. So we made the trip there. Derek kept insisting that the malaria injection was the worst, like really painful, straight into the stomach, agonising. We queued up, I feared the worst - all tense again - got the jab, which, much to my relief (to say the least) was not directly into the stomach, and back we went to planning. It was going to happen! Hard to believe but we believed it.

Someone mentioned that if we were going to pass through any number of countries we would have to have what they called a Camping Carnet. We had no idea what that was, but were told to go to the Automobile Association on London Road in Stanmore because that is where Camping Carnets were issued. We went. We told the gentleman there about what we planned to do. When he picked himself up off the floor, he looked bewildered, shook his head, muttered to himself, and then said, "Well, if that's what you're going to do, just go." We took his word for it, and later on would learn what the consequences can be, just taking someone's word for it. All the same, I started to dare to imagine, having really nothing to go by. We had also obtained salt tablets, advised that we would lose a lot of salt through sweating in the desert heat. Plus a couple of sandwiches, and a box of bullet shaped cigar-like aluminium tubes full of Nulacyn, for my ulcers, and nothing else of much consequence. We were as ready as we'd ever be.

The local paper was invited to do a story on our departure. And there we are, two young men with no idea, not even of what it is like setting out to sea on a ferry. All I knew of water was the Lake, no longer my place, though in my heart it will perhaps always be 'my place'. The reporter came, equipped with the necessary props, a map, which happened to be of Wales - we had made one journey to Wales, as a test run, to see if the car could get that far because if it could get to Wales, well, it was just roads between St Albans and New Zealand. We'd just need oil and petrol. We spread the map out on the bonnet of the car. Guy takes the photo and a few days later we're in the papers. My first and last headline. Front page, bottom left: "The Explorers: Will They Return?" Strange. We didn't plan to return. After all, we were driving to New Zealand, weren't we. We might have looked intrepid but the truth is we probably just looked like two naïve 20 year olds embarking on what could be anything from the trip of a lifetime to a death sentence. No one, the man from the *Herts Advertiser* told us, no one from this district has ever crossed the Sahara in a Ford Prefect. "And good luck, gentlemen. You're going to need it." Why would anyone want to cross the Sahara desert in a Ford Prefect anyway? Well, because it was there, and because the Ford Prefect was all we had. Was I scared before we left? My youth had been scary, much of the time. Yes, I had been terrified. But you adapt to circumstances. But I had now, in my hands, a plan that would make the world of difference: it was my plan, or our plan, not someone else knocking us into shape. Yes, I did feel a little sick, the day we left. A little scared? No, not really. We had no idea what we were getting ourselves into. And that was starting to make its impression on us: we had no idea where we were going! And then we laughed. Would we ever have any idea where we are going? We'll set off and find out. Simple.

We really didn't have much of any consequence. But what was to unfold was of a consequence I still feel, and contains moments that are more precious the further they recede into the distance of the ground covered. It would be a journey that changed everything, and no harm done, and all achieved with a smile and an open hand.

We filled the tank, and checked the oil, and had enough air in the tyres. And we set off. Sunday, August 25th 1962. Gentlemen, start your engine. Wave goodbye to no one in particular, down through St Albans, past Woolworths and Halfords and the Clock Tower which had been there eight or nine hundred years - and would still be there if we ever got back - past Thompson and Debenhams, stop at an intersection or two, and off down the A5 (the old Roman road), and goodbye Verulanium. Windows open, summer air blowing through. "Want a sandwich, Degs?" "What you talking about! We haven't gone five miles yet!" Whistle, doze, engine sounded good. Share the driving and first stop Dover. We hoped.

# CHAPTER 2:

# The thin dotted line

*(England and France had changed hands several times over the centuries and many a soul had died in the contest over what belonged to whom. For a while they shared a common official language, and then disputed which language was the best. Between them the two countries had meddled with other countries far, far away, and created problems that would take centuries to sort out, if ever. But for quite a while, and relatively recently, after the Entente-Cordiale of 1904, England and France had been on friendly terms. That process had taken 1000 years. Whatever Derek and I would find in North Africa was living history.)*

To secure my first journey in a car I'd said goodbye to that beautiful Moto-Rumi, and that near broke my heart. We had £320 cash between us, in our money belts, normally enough to last two people two months. But what we were about to do was apparently not normal. We had no way of knowing. Two young men off to see the world, and we weren't conscripts.

Every organised expedition has its inventory. We didn't. But there was a lot of stuff packed in the car, which was polished for the off, a picture perfect showroom gleam.

2 passports (brand new)
Certificates of injections
1 guitar, so that we could entertain along the way, or busk if we got really desperately short of cash
1 Perdio radio
1 Bukta tent
2 sleeping bags
1 single ring Gaz cooker
2 tin plates
2 tin mugs
1 carton of Nulacyn tubes
2 cartons of Ovaltine biscuits
1 box of salt tablets
1 bag of sandwiches
1 very small red notebook from Woolworths and a pen
4 toothbrushes and toothpaste
2 jars of Brylcreem for imagined nights out on the town somewhere
Assorted clothes, including my Burton's suit, shirts, jeans, shorts and t-shirts
1 Indian beaded belt (it was the 60s!)
Shoes/boots/sandals
1 sheet of petrol coupons
3 spare fan belts
2 gallons of motor oil, oil filters, spare spark plugs, contact points, rotor arms, distributor caps, grease gun, spanners,

insulating tape, wire, and odds and ends that might help get us out of a spot of bother, mechanically.

We hadn't yet bought a map of anywhere. I didn't have a full driver's licence. Derek did. That was another risk: we'd share the driving, and hope our luck held out.

My first world was home and school. Unacceptable but inescapable. Not good for the health either. My first freedom was the Lake District: perfectly OK, and me just being myself. That kind of held me together, allowed me to gather strength, not to mention stocking up on peace of mind, and just be a kid poking around with a stick, dreaming, discovering whatever was there to be found and bothered by no one. But sooner or later I would have to desert that freedom and re-enter the first world. Doing that doesn't cure ulcers. But now, at near twenty-one years old, I was setting out to claim my second world, just mine, the real world, on my terms and whatever the world gave me or threw at me. It was almost delicious, moving and taking the initiative because I wanted to and not because I was on the run back-peddling out of harm's way. A few concerned folk warned us of the risks, and with very good reason: they knew, and we had no idea. We heard them, not really paying attention, and ignored them. What could be more dangerous and risky than the years I had already survived? After that, anything, I told myself, would be water off a duck's back - been there done that kind of thing. Anyway the family unit was disintegrating like a clearing log jam.

Mum and dad had set up independently, and I couldn't see myself in either of the new camps, and so the timing of the emigration was just right, even natural, even inevitable. A clean break. I heard myself saying, "Den, go for it!" and I went. For Derek, the motivation was not the same. I was about to have my first proof that you only really get to know someone when you live together by choice, cheek by jowl. Up until now I had had no choice, given my personality, than to put on a brave face: I was an extrovert out of necessity, perhaps desperation. Derek was, well, shall we say, introverted. We made a good balanced pair. He was the senior partner, four to five years older than me, reliable, organised, fastidiously tidy, and totally loyal. Sometimes you say about someone that you'd trust them with your life; for me he was that kind of person. We had a great and quiet confidence in each other. I had a full head of hair; he was already losing his. I was kind of naturally cheeky, ready for a laugh, a little bravado, to make the school bullies laugh. I was always skinny, but worked hard at the gym and always stayed on the wiry side; Derek was taller and had more fat on him than I did.

Seeing the white cliffs of Dover disappear was very moving, the first time I had left those shores. From the Lake District to the Channel, that's already a journey: the expanses of water were getting bigger. What lay on the other side of the Channel was as blank for us as your knowledge of what is going to happen on the next page. And sooner than we expected, the Ford Prefect had rolled down the ramp and we were in Calais, and driving on the wrong side of the road, that is to say, the right side. Heaven help us. We headed straight for Paris. The countryside was so much wider than anything I had ever seen. You could see further and there was more space between places: there were no hedges. Long winding tree-lined roads and some as straight as arrows, and cars like the rear-engine Renault Dauphine, Citroen saloons, black Citroens straight out of Maigret, and of course that charmer, the pretty Citroen 2CV. Some I had seen in war movies, but never with my own eyes. And there, proudly amongst all the romance of the road, our beige Ford Prefect humming along, LXD-521. It didn't know of course, but that machine was being asked to get us to New Zealand. (I often wonder what happened to it, so if you ever see that number plate, please let me know!)

Basically by trial and error, passing the same landmarks a few times, round and round, being hooted at, fists waving through open windows (I can't imagine why), we manage to navigate around Paris and eventually arrive at Fontainebleau, in the countryside south-east of the city, find a cheap campsite, and get ourselves set for the night. I was already starting to feel the pinch. I only had a few cigarettes left and had resigned myself to the horrible truth that the budget would not cater to replenishing supplies. Maybe it wouldn't be too hard to bum one now and again. Might be the only choice.

And that was our first night away from our homeland. Having put a unique distance between myself and life until yesterday, I reflected a little as we drove further south. Not long ago, we had moved from Blacksmiths Lane after mum and dad accepted the offer of a council house on Francis Avenue, New Greens Estate, but still in St Albans. It was an improvement. A nice house with garden back and front, three bedrooms, and stepping up in the world we then had a real gas stove to replace the coal or wood fired black-lead range on which food had been cooked every day up until then. The gas stove had a meter and needed feeding with pennies, which stopped people like us from running up bills we couldn't pay. Conveniently it was just a couple of minutes walk from Townsend secondary modern school, in those days when education was as class divided as the rest of England. I'd been born on the wrong side of the railway tracks, as had probably a good half of the children in England. Not long before we set out, mum and dad separated anyway. Changes, changes.

*The Ancient Briton* had become my local pub, for a couple of pints of mild, a few games of darts with my many friends, and that was a happy evening. Amongst those friends was Ted, almost old enough to be my dad. He was a builder but was always very smartly dressed when off work. Brogues, Gabardine trousers, cutaway collar, Windsor knot in his tie - very smart. He knew we were heading off on a journey down through Europe and told us he was going to Milan for a holiday.

"Why don't you meet me at Milan Cathedral and have a bit of a tour and a glass?"

"OK. Sounds good. Don't be late."

We fixed the day and time. September 5th around 5PM.

You live where you're brought up. There isn't a choice. You find beauty there. It becomes what you know and what helps shape you, and it leaves an impression. What is new to your eye always looks more beautiful perhaps than to those who live within the beauty that you see for the first time. And to me, driving through this landscape I could not have imagined, well, I was stunned. So many small and attractive villages, everything laid out quite differently, built in a different way, and the expanse. On top of that, the weather was warm, and getting warmer the further south we went. I know that's obvious, but you don't notice much of a difference between St Albans and south London. We quickly became efficient at making and breaking camp and the car was running smooth as you like. Nothing flash like the newer Citroens or as charming as the older Citroens with their canvas seats on springs. The Ford engine was elementary but in its way ideal. A simple carburator, side valve, four pistons, oil pumped around effectively, and everything in the engine was accessible, unlike sophisticated modern cars where you can't fit as much as a cigarette paper under the bonnet. The Ford Prefect was working like a treat.

New landscapes, new experiences. From now on, everything for Derek and myself would be a new experience and we wouldn't have time to get used to one before we were moving on to the next. It was at a campsite outside Lyon. Very civilised, with clean showers. At home we just had a bath. Here there was a shower. And that was the first shower of my young life. A wonderfully long shower. A real luxury. We left early in the morning, around dawn: we had to pay by the hour, and every franc saved was food further down the track. And on we went, through Chambery and climbing up and over the Alps. Another first. Never before had I had to get out of a car in order to see down into a valley. Incredible feeling. And with all the hairpin bends on the way down, the brakes were getting hot but they didn't let us down too fast and we made good progress towards Torino where we stopped for fuel. You learn the tricks of your neighbourhood. In very cold countries, do not put your bare hands on a car door handle in the middle of a snow storm in winter: they will stick and you won't be able to get them unstuck. In France and most places in the world, it's best to drive on the same side of the road as everything else going your way. In Italy .... You learn the hard way often enough. After sitting in a hot car for hours, and you're sweating and stiff, it's natural to want to stretch the legs and cool off. There we were in the petrol station forecourt. The car has stopped. I am very keen to get out. I had taken my shoes off some time ago. I open the door quickly and I step out, barefoot, onto the tarmac. I jumped back into the car like a jack in the box going in reverse, and fast. The soles of my feet! Ouch! To compensate myself for the pain I enjoyed a huge slice of melon, fresh and cool red and green and juicy. Derek had one too but he ate it in a slightly different mood than I ate mine. I imagined my tongue was the sole of my foot.

We aimed for Milan, which is hard to miss even for a novice. The huge Milan cathedral (five centuries to build, but still incomplete, with the last gate only being put in place three years after we passed through) with all its thin little spires and on top somewhere among the figures,

Madonna, and Napoleon, King of Italy. All that history and grandeur put the stumpy Clock Tower and Cathedral of St Albans well into the shade of an England already out of sight but not yet completely out of mind. The heat was phenomenal, and the eyes feasted on everything that the scene revealed: massive melons on the market stalls in the square, very impressive, and the birds were worth looking at too, for two young Englishmen pushed out into the Italian sun, and not really aware of what was happening. "Hey Den. Look at that!" Two young men fresh out of jail, under a glaring sun, probably looking like escapees as well, gazing at the impossible dream. Couldn't chat them up because we didn't know any Italian. We just gazed. Wow! Look at her! We'd forgotten the melons and the heat.

We waited and waited. It was September 5th, and it was not long before 3PM. Waiting wasn't a problem, with so much to look at, beautiful cafes full of people relaxing and laughing, the fascinating sounds and smells, but sitting on the steps of the cathedral was becoming uncomfortable once 3PM had passed and we settled on a café we spotted and ordered coffee just off the cathedral square. And there we sat under the sunshade like proper rich men, and we watched and listened. Americans, English people, Germans, people who spoke languages I didn't know existed. The whole world seemed to be strolling past, no one in a hurry. Bliss. Girls on the backs of Lambrettas, often side-saddle, holding their skirts down, or not. Great stuff. All so pleasant. But there's only so much the eyes can absorb, so we walked back over to the Cathedral steps, and waited and began to get restless.

My friend Ted wasn't going to show up. (I never did see him again. I heard later on that he had moved to Ireland to build another house.) Ah well, never mind. We'd seen Milan and it was worth seeing too.

I was now doing spells of the driving, once outside big towns and cities like Genova on the coast, Monaco, Nice and Cannes. We did have a map by now and it was open on his knees, while those hours gave him a chance to relax and take in the scenery which we might never see again. But Derek was at the wheel when we hit Monte Carlo. Den Logan and Derek Jakeman, experienced circuit board solderers recently retired from Murphy Radio Welwyn Garden, now in Monte Carlo? Ridiculous. Who would have thought? But there we were. Two big gamblers out taking a spin. What an incredible world we live on, once you start lifting the lid of this Pandora's box! You could feel the wealth, with a stream of flash cars, people dressed up like I couldn't believe, and in that context our by now very dusty beige Ford Prefect looked like a dust cart, a relic of some unsophisticated past, much like the one we had come from. We strolled, breathing it in: some might rub off. The marina - my eyes popped! - the gin palaces, yachts of all shapes and sizes, gorgeous, drop dead beautiful birds in bikinis on deck. Two kids in the most tempting sweet shop I could imagine. I was so stage struck that I kept tripping over my own feet.

"We can't come to Monte Carlo and not have a flutter, Degs."

"No one would believe us if we said we'd just driven through. Let's have a look."

We picked what must be the main casino, which meant the biggest and the flashiest one. A staircase led up to the main doors, outside which stood two men in stage-set livery, including top hats. We agreed: just a look around and a Coke, just for the hell of it. The doorman held open the door for us, not trying that hard to hide the disapproving look on his face but not stopping us from going in. We knew we were riffraff and could live with that and I never could imagine myself in a top hat - though I could imagine myself on deck on one of those yachts. Girlfriend in bikini and me with my martini? Yes, I could handle that.

Up until that moment, just after we got into the place, I had believed our new council house home on Francis Avenue was big. At least it was a step up in the right direction. But my eyes looked around, and my eyes went up to the ceiling and saw a chandelier (I had never seen one before) that, if not as big as the house on Francis Avenue, must have cost a whole lot more. It was simply huge. And beneath it drifted the world's rich and famous like cherries in a cocktail glass: women in tiaras, evening gowns, high heels, and jewellery just one piece of which would have funded our trip several times over - I didn't even have enough for fags! We swaggered into the Long Bar, and, getting into the mood, we put our money on the table.

"Two medium cokes, please." (Bold as you like.)

"Eight shillings and six pence, sir." (Not sarcastic but not very impressed.)

My mind screamed, "How much!!" And I heard the echo, "Eight shillings and six pence, sir." Derek blushed and his neck shrank into his shoulders a little ways. At home that would have cost six pence. But you're only young once and so we bit the bullet and sipped, slowly, little sips, dainty like, meaning to show that we had all the time in the world and we would spend our fortune at our own pace.

"Cheers, Degs."

"Cheers, Den. Let's take our time."

We soaked up the atmosphere. We'd paid good money to soak up atmosphere. New boys on the block. Look at me and eat your heart out. This Coke just cost me a whole day's wages! I don't know where she came from, but as if by magic this slim, slim woman was sitting beside me at the bar, perhaps thirty years old, and then another one just as jaw dropping appeared beside Derek. The difference between twenty-one years old and twenty-five years old doesn't sound much, but at twenty five years old you are perhaps more confident than at twenty one, especially with a woman with legs so long, oh such very long legs and shapely too. Derek's eyes were trying to find somewhere to hide. I was getting dizzy. The perfume! The smile! I thought, "If she touches me, I am going to fuse to my chair like a piece of solder." We said, "Hi", real casual, and drank down the rest of the Coke. We said "Bye" and, calm as you like (oh yes), excused ourselves. We went out through the main doors in a daze. The doorman in the top hat looked relieved to see us go. We paused on the steps. I gave Derek a questioning look. He shook his head. I could hear him thinking, "Not enough in the kitty, Den. You know that." Someone had to be in control. It wasn't me. The sunlight was very bright. I let out a slow breath. Would I ever come down to earth? Phew.

Derek drives. I drive. Beautiful scenery, blue sea, beaches. The Riviera, Toulon, Marseille, Montpelier, Perpignan. I drive. Derek drives. Monte Carlo's an unforgettable memory. Border crossing into Spain, and then Barcelona where we stopped. The temperature kept going up and the car was getting more and more thirsty, and petrol stations were fewer and further between. So we bought a couple of canvas five-gallon WW2 water bags and hung one each from each side of the car, on the outside door handles. And then we just kept moving. Anywhere we stopped we would have to spend money, and Egypt (not to mention New Zealand) was still a long way off and our budget was still a long way off any luxuries - those two Cokes had set us back. We kept moving. As long as the engine was running we were moving towards New Zealand and we weren't spending more money than we had to. If you keep driving along southern Spain you will pass through Valencia, Alicante and Almeria, and eventually you'll get to Gibraltar, which is just what we did.

Our plan was to get on a boat and land in North Africa. Nice idea, but no, not quite that simple.

"You'll have to go to the British Embassy. You have to have a permit to go across to North Africa. There's been a war on."

Monte Carlo. Tiaras. Long legs. Yachts. War? What was going on in the world?! With the French-Algeria uprising barely settled, apparently the British Embassy required us to hear a few words. More often than not, what are deemed to be important buildings look important as well. The British Embassy in Gibraltar was no exception. Impressive building. Feeling a little dwarfed inside. Third door on the right, sir, and sit and wait. We found it, went in, and sat. It was pleasant and cool. We waited, perhaps ten or fifteen minutes. A door opened. An important looking gentleman came in, carrying a folder. Important looking gentlemen often carry folders. I never have carried a folder and that is because I am not an important looking gentleman. He was. He sat down behind his desk and put the folder down.

"Draw up a chair, gentlemen."

We drew up chairs. I felt I was back in school.

"Good afternoon, Mr. Logan, Mr. Jakeman, and welcome to Gibraltar. What exactly are your plans? What route are you going to take?"

We explained. It was very basic.

"Ah, yes, that's just as I thought. Well, it's a little complicated over there. It's not quite like driving up the A1. And I am sorry to have to advise you that, well, our advice is not to go. It's too dangerous."

We looked at each other and felt sick. All this way just to go all the way back? Our faces obviously told him that we had planned to go through North Africa and that was that.

"But if you are determined to go, then you will have to sign this document."

He opened the folder. There was only one piece of paper in it, with its carbon copy. He took it, turned it around and politely pushed it across the desk so that we could read it.

"Basically, when you sign that, you are releasing the British Government from any responsibility for your safety, and I have to stress that that means *any* responsibility. Once you have signed it, once you are on the boat to Morocco, then what happens to you is entirely at your own risk. You will not be able to claim or expect any protection as British citizens. You have just come through France. In Algeria they won't appreciate that. Have a good think. If, for example ….."

And he kept on talking as we read the document signing our lives away. We had broken free of Murphy Radio, broken free of St Albans, left the lake District, escaped the wonderful temptations of Monte Carlo, and now we had to decide whether or not we wanted to break completely free of the British Empire. Sounds like a big step. To us, it was just signing a piece of paper and handing it back. Derek and I looked at each other. We knew we were not going anywhere except Egypt and then New Zealand.

"Do you have a pen, sir?"

We signed on the thin dotted line.

"But before you leave, gentleman, I have to repeat the warning I have already given you, and ask you to very carefully consider the facts. It is very, very dangerous over there. Even if I was armed I wouldn't go. The military are still in place. There has been fighting and there is still some fighting going on. There is no one there to protect you. Tanks are still in place. It's a military zone. You are just two young men with a Ford Prefect, some clothes and two water bags. The British Government would advise you not to go."

We thanked him and politely pushed the signed document back towards him. As he did not seem to want to pick it up, we pushed our chairs back a little, and waited for him to give us our copy of the document. We thanked him again for making the situation clear to us, shook his hand, turned around and found our own way out of the building. Strangely I didn't feel concerned.

Out on the street, I put my hand on Derek's shoulder.

"We'll get through, Degs. And if we don't, well, what a way to go out, hey!"

He smiled, and not nervously. But neither of us felt gung-ho. We were simply and modestly resolute. Go back? Not on your life.

It was comforting being in Gibraltar. The place was oddly like home, with the London coppers (policemen) - it was, after all, Empire. We met lots of English people, all of whom, without exception, thought we were "totally mad". No one wanted to come with us. We found a NAAFI, like an armed forces café, and had bacon sandwiches and a pot of tea. Bloody great. Fed and watered we set off to the docks. North Africa, you ain't seen nothing yet.

# CHAPTER 3:

# Excuse me, which way is Tunisia?

*(Morocco - Maroc: Both the French and the Spanish controlled the country until it broke free from years of French colonial rule with the return of King Mohammed V in 1956 from his exile in Madagascar and Corsica and the proclamation of Morocco's independence on November 18th, 1956. By 1958 the Spanish were also negotiated out of the areas they had control of, and the country was ruled as a constitutional monarchy. In 1961 King Hassan II was crowned king, after which there would be a period of tension and unrest.)*

## *The Kasbah*

"Two single tickets to Tangier for us, and one for the vehicle, please."

We showed the 'release document' and our passports.

"So, looks like you gentlemen are on your own. Keep your heads down."

We smiled and soon were walking the decks. The journey took perhaps two hours. All the way, dolphins trailed along behind the ship, darting this way and that, leaping, streaming along with their silver skins glistening in the sunlight close to the surface. We saw flying fish, and not a cloud in the sky. We had not see rain for days. Behind the sales counter at Halfords several months earlier I had stood and tried to imagine what Africa would look like. A rind of brown and not a tree in sight. Of course it is impossible to imagine. But I stood on the deck and looked as Africa pushed its way through the Mediterranean and into our lives and there it was, a brown mass looming on the horizon, a rind of brown and not a tree in sight. It wasn't cleanly breathtaking like the Alps; it wasn't enchanting like the tree lined roads of France; it wasn't the glitz and glitter of Monte Carlo. It was a long brown treeless mass.

"It can't all be like that, surely."

For the second time we disembarked. Europe and now Africa. Whatever lay ahead was completely out of our experience and no one, not even the British Government, to call on in emergencies. Neither of us had been at that level of independence before and neither of us had a clue what it might entail. The landscape, the languages - though we would recognise English and French now and again - and the laws of the land, all a completely blank book about to be filled in. We queued up in the line of vehicles waiting to drive off the ferry: a motley collection, with big, new and old American jeeps, fancy saloon cars, strong, solidly built things that could handle the roads (whatever they were like), and amongst them this humble Ford Prefect, discreetly camouflaged in beige, the fearless dune-hopper from St Albans, and already twelve years old.

The word 'busy' conjured up images of heavy traffic, national holiday weekends, London. This place was busy, a different busy to the one I knew. Donkeys, goats, camels, and people on foot, always moving, stopping, looking, this way and that way, everybody selling something to someone. Sunshine, colours and bustle. We carefully negotiated the narrow streets, pausing for goats, declining a sales pitch through the open windows, and looking at the backside of camels and just seeing a section of their lower legs and flanks through the windows. There was a constantly changing smell of food being cooked, the sight of carpets hanging everywhere there was space to hang something. We had a couple of very slow motion bumps, and probably there was some lone donkey going home with the Ford insignia stamped on its bum. We had quickly forgotten the brown treeless mass after the blue blue sea. The sight of water has a very positive effect. We were fascinated and parked the car when a suitable space turned up. We did not forget to lock the car up: inside it was all we had, except for the money belts tucked under our t-shirts. This wasn't Woolworths. It was an Aladdin's cave without walls and the sky for a roof. The eyes were busy, not looking for anything in particular but very curious. Being of limited resources we 'window-shopped' but did buy some fruit and some local biscuits. By the time we arrived back at the car, would you believe, there's a parking ticket on the windscreen. It was a sweet feeling, though, out of the bustle of the kasbah, tearing up the ticket and stuffing the pieces in my pocket. Very

## The Lane via Benghazi

soon we would be gone without trace into the deserts of North Africa. First stop Ceuta and through Tetoutan and onto the coast road as far as Alexandria, the Pearl of the Mediterranean. We made camp, our first night in Africa.

The tent was proving a good buy: built in ground sheet, plenty of room for two single sleeping bags and still space for other stuff. We sat outside with our coffee and Arabic flat bread to go with the tinned meat. It dawned on both of us, that this was a momentous night in our lives. Certainly not Dr. Livingstone and Stanley, nor Scott of the Antarctic, and we weren't New World settlers persecuted into another landscape. But our lives had changed already, just as our concept of living in the world had changed, not to mention our concept of each other. The closer you have to live together, the more space you need to allow each other. We didn't have to leap about, but we were thrilled, we were excited, we were full of anticipation, and we could say we, Derek and Den, had made it to Africa of our own free will.

Where had I come from? A mixed youth, a few bruises, a lot of good friends, Metalwork and English Literature, gofer in a solicitor's office, briefly employed by Murphy Radio and not fast-tracked for fame and fortune. And yet I was taking charge of me, having declined to follow the advise of Her Majesty's representative in Gibraltar. I had heard the voice saying, "Go for it, Den" and myself and Derek had gone for it, and here we were, in Morocco, Africa, and that was something no one and nothing could ever take away from us. We told each other there was a very long way to go yet, but I did not know what a very long way meant: we had already come a very long way so how long was a long way yet? I was learning it has nothing to do with distance. Both Derek and I could now say that we had created a dream and had accomplished Stage 1 - St Albans to Morocco - and, so far, there had been no mishaps. Looking back on even that short time since driving down the A5 was a source of real strength, and there is an almost unbelievable security in translating all the talk into the action, despite the scepticism of others and despite official warnings that perhaps we were quite mad. I could respect myself, and I could comfort and reassure myself. Whether life would respect, comfort and reassure me remained to be seen. I knew that I might imagine there was plenty of time: there isn't. I might have imagined that tomorrow never comes: it had - I was living in it. Before turning in, I put a bottle of milk with a secure metal lid outside the tent, along with half the packet of biscuits we had bought in Tangier. If we left them inside the tent we might knock the bottle over or roll and crush the biscuits. We went to sleep feeling pleased, relieved, and a little awe-struck. Things were looking good.

## *Smile for the Camera*

That was a good night's sleep. But things weren't looking so good when I unzipped the tent, just to set eyes on the milk and biscuits. They had gone. And the long trail of large retreating termites indicated in which direction the biscuits disappeared. The vanishing milk was a mystery. We had our coffee anyway and packed up the tent. That disturbed three scorpions which stood their ground, like spear-throwers poised to attack. We were on their territory and they were going to defend it if they had to. A long way from the timid newt we'd have seen in England. Africa was making itself felt. Expect the unexpected. But we weren't reading the signs. Warnings appear and somehow you don't pay attention. Derek went to take things to the car only five metres away and noticed that the driver's door handle had been broken off during the night - the only door that locked with a key. After that we secured the car doors at night by tying strong string to the passenger door handle inside the car and feeding the other end through the boot. That would mean using the boot key to open the boot, pull the string to open the passenger door. A nuisance. Whoever had taken the milk was perhaps looking for the coffee and sugar as well! We had slept so well we hadn't heard a sound, even that close. Obviously a person or persons unknown had been walking around us during the night, and we hadn't so much as turned over in our sleep. There is a huge difference between a well-appointed French campsite with showers and camping on the side of the road in Morocco. We were a little more on our guard.

Routine pre-departure check: oil, fine; water in radiator, fine. And off towards Melilla close to the Algerian border. We were sure we were on the coast road. It followed the coast for a while and then turned inland, and then back to the coast, so it must be the coast road. The road itself was a moveable feast as well. One minute it was there, and next minute it had gone somewhere else without us. Weird. You had to concentrate all the time because the road disappeared beneath sand blown across it. Derek said something about being more careful because if we left the road and lost it we too would be covered in sand. Were we getting desert wise? Not really. We were still in the novelty stage. We still hadn't seen a sand-storm - what would that be like?

As the road moved towards, and along and away from the coast, the temperature went up and down noticeably, and quite early on it would be anywhere from 38-45 degrees, and no air-conditioning for us. Our eyes were getting accustomed to the terrain and the hot air. Both had a monotony and concentration is a trial. To try and alleviate the monotony of the heat, we would wind the windscreen up, like a flap, so that air passed underneath it and into the car. The downside of that strategy was that anything airborne came in as well and as fast as the air did, and a few fat flying insects hitting your face at speed is painful, and sometimes messy which might be why rally drivers wear helmets and goggles. Now why hadn't we thought of that?

Out on the open road, it made little difference where we camped. During that day we might have seen two or three cars and a battered bus, packed with passengers inside and a herd of goats on top. So we camped anywhere because one spot was as good as the next and none of them had a shower anyway and we were starting to feel grubby. On the other hand we didn't have to put coins in a slot to pay for the overnight stay so we felt we were being very economical. The next morning we would arrive at the Moroccan-Algerian border crossing at Oujda.

•

*(Algeria had been controlled by France since 1848, as a military colony. By 1947 it had been declared a part of France, and all Algerians were treated as French citizens. The very bitter struggle for independence had turned into armed resistance in 1954 with the uprising. After years of guerilla warfare, including acts of sabotage in France, independence was finally achieved on 5 July 1962. However, the situation was still volatile and French troops stationed in Algeria continued to stay there and it was not until 1964 - two years after our journey through Algeria - that the French military had left the country.)*

We had already passed through a few international borders - France-Switzerland, Switzerland-Italy, Italy-France, France-Spain, Spain-Gibraltar, and all of them fairly routine. The Customs officials were civilians. Greeting. Show passport. Face gets checked. Car gets a look over. Stamped passport. Back in the car and off we would go. Yes, but what has happened so far does not necessarily prepare you at all for what happens next. (The broken car door handle was a reminder about that. Roads that vanish spontaneously were also a reminder of that.) I could remember those prisoners of war in the Lake district of St Albans, and the German who put my tyre back on. (I could remember my gun collection, too, and the fascination that the metal and wood construction, the smell and the mechanics of a gun had held for me.) I could remember parades, like the Trooping of the Colour. I had seen some war-movies. But never had I been surrounded by professional soldiers or seen modern weapons held in a way that indicated someone would kill me and Derek, if they had to. Loaded guns aimed at you are not fascinating.

It was a rude shock. There were clearly a lot of things I had never seen. And, ready or not, here came another one.

The area was swarming with heavily armed soldiers. Berets, black boots, guns at the ready, eyes that pinned you against the scenery like drawing pins. They escorted us across the courtyard to the Customs Inspector's window. We handed over our passports. This was Algeria. We had recently passed through France. The French were not welcome here in Algeria. The English and the French had at least one thing in common: they were colonialists against whom certain countries had decided to rebel. Algeria had rebelled. We were white. We were young, and perhaps braver than for our own good, or for theirs for that matter. The air was brittle with tension.

"You English? What you do here Algeria? Where to?"

He was not happy, not at all happy. Didn't the country have enough problems without two young English making matters worse!

Between us, Derek and I tried to slowly explain the inspiring journey we were on. You know, sir, Algeria, Tunisia, Libya, Alexandria in Egypt, and, yes, New Zealand some time after that. We were simply in transit to somewhere else. Algeria, to us, was no more than a landscape to cross. Algeria to them was someone to die for if you had to.

He didn't seem very impressed, and he was certainly less than inspired. In fact, he became very officious. Not someone you would want to upset. It didn't sound good. He had another long, long look at our passports, and then gestured for two soldiers to come forward. Every question was menacing. I could see the face of the man at the Embassy in Gibraltar and heard his voice saying "a war's been going on....must ask you to reconsider...." And here we were and not feeling very welcome. We had reached the edge of a pit: who would push us in?

"Camera? Where's camera?" says the soldier about to search me.

"Gun. Where's your guns?" says the soldier searching Derek.

We don't have a camera or guns. They are not playing around. They are serious and possibly deadly serious, and I had never felt like I did then. We obviously couldn't say anything to each other as that would only have provoked them, and they were already on the edge. With every inch of my body that was being examined, the soldier was touching memories of earlier struggles, spots where I had been hit before, often, spots I had forgotten, but this unknown man with a rifle and black boots could do things to me that dad could not have imagined. I don't think I was shaking, but my memories were vibrating inside me. Derek was probably wishing he was still soldering circuit boards. I knew we had nothing to fear so long as we took them seriously and helped them do whatever they had to do - apart from helping them shoot us. I didn't feel brave. I felt worried? Scared? Out of my depth? Maybe all those. Terrified? Possibly. But we didn't have a camera and we didn't have guns. But they didn't believe us. They seemed mostly concerned about us having a camera.

"I have said, we don't have camera. We just have some clothes, our tent (gestures, slowly) and guitar (more gestures, but avoiding the risk of smiling)." And then I showed my empty hands. Not in surrender; just quietly to claim our innocence.

"The car." It was an order. My stomach dropped. Lambs to the slaughter.

We walked out into the sun and watched four soldiers empty the car, and I mean empty the car. Everything, and what had been in a bag was emptied out, carefully and deliberately, until what had been in the car was spread out on the ground beside the car. They then emptied the boot, along with the spare wheel and tools, but they still weren't satisfied. We knew we had nothing to fear being found; we knew what our intentions were. They didn't trust the piece of string. They didn't trust our gestures and they didn't trust anyone who had recently been through France. Why hadn't we thought about that before now? Well, we assumed, as you do, that what you have known is going to continue: it doesn't. Derek opened the bonnet for them and stood back, at a short distance, where he was watched closely by another soldier. Yet another soldier checked over the engine - it wasn't difficult because you could see around the engine very easily. (Thank you, Mr. Ford!) And once again they asked us where the camera was. We said once again that we did not have a camera but being very careful not to sound impatient or challenging: there's no point in shouting the truth. Still not convinced, they checked under the car, feeling all over and tapping, and crawling out from under it again. They hadn't found anything, but, still eyeing us with marked suspicion, they allowed the Customs Official to stamp our passports. So much had been made of the camera they hoped to find, and so thoroughly had they looked for one, that I am sure, had they found one, they might easily have shot us, and you wouldn't be reading this. The termites would have taken us off into the desert as well, helped by heaven knows what. It might have taken a while but termites are not pressed for time. And the Embassy man's words kept cruising through my brain as if they were looking for a place to park ...."have to ask you .... reconsider.....no responsibility for your safety .... on your own."

Before we got on our way, we filled the radiator with water, and poured another can of petrol into the fuel tank. We now had one can left. After getting through that border post, we both knew we were well and truly on our own, and that we had only just passed into Algeria. We now had to get out of Algeria. The Ford Prefect looked so humble. We packed the car, without rushing and feeling annoyed or indignant, and headed off. There was some comfort in being surrounded by our stuff again, and by the empty desert landscape, and just us. We didn't feel like saying much. But Derek did whisper. "Welcome to Algeria, Den. It's a relief that didn't turn nasty."

## *Don't speak too soon*

When we had set off down the A5, we did so without any notion of holiday in our thinking. It was no more and no less than a journey and not once had we entertained the notion of 'going back', not in the conversations between us and not when talking about the venture to someone else. We did not need an end date: holidays usually have a return date, an end date. We didn't actually have a destination, no thought of arriving anywhere and stopping for good.

We were just heading towards the land of the long white cloud and taking the very long way round. New Zealand made some kind of sense. They spoke English, sheep were common, and we had sheep in England, and so being there would be to arrive somewhere vaguely familiar. And besides, they played rugby and cricket. Then why not Australia? Maybe we thought it was too big. St Albans is a small town, not a big city. Blacksmiths Lane was literally a lane and Francis Avenue was a minor common or garden street. We weren't city kids. And we weren't gung-ho.

One group of soldiers at the relative safety of a border crossing is one thing. I had never once thought of defending myself violently, my only tactic in defending myself against dad having been to bob and weave, timing a run, ducking. Until the day before, I had never had a gun thrust in my face. But now we were officially inside the country those shocks were well gone and we hoped to be peacefully heading for Oran and the capital of Alger. Military vehicles would pass us this way and that at irregular intervals. It kept us on edge and we were not used to that. Then I heard Derek mumble, "Oh no. Here we go." I looked. It was something like a checkpoint on the road, soldiers either side, weapons at the ready. We slowed down. Four jeeps, soldiers armed to the teeth, and on active duty. Rifles, pistols, machine guns. Well, I joke to myself, if they think that's impressive, wait until they take the full force of my loaded guitar. Let's see how they handle that. Nice joke, white boy, nice joke.

The soldiers are either side of and in front of and behind the car, rifles cocked. With the end of his gun, one soldier tells us to get out. We get out and one soldier either side closes the doors. A senior soldier, maybe a sergeant, strolls over. Big chest, a professional soldier. What he has seen I hate to think. I am not feeling very comfortable about what Derek and I are about to see. Neither of us knew from experience what it means to 'lose your nerve', and until that moment neither of us knew what 'vulnerable' could mean. Yesterday had been gentle practice, a first lesson, a getting to know you, a softening up. We were soft. The sergeant spoke in broken English - travellers, be grateful for small mercies.

"American?"

Stuttering and quivering were two words I had never had to use before. Before I could answer, I knew I was going to stutter, and, though not a coward, I knew I was about to quiver. But I was still putting on a brave face.

"No, sir, English. On our way to Egypt."

He looked straight into my eyes. It was like looking into a bright glaring light.

"Camera? Guns?"

"No, no. Sir." I could feel my buttocks clamp together. I didn't now want to allow the dull brown sand between my feet to turn a dark liquid tan. I didn't want to be humiliated. What I wanted to say was, "Look, for heaven's sake. We've been through this ritual already with your friends back there. They've searched us and the car, and we have the stamps in our passports to prove it. We don't have a camera and we don't have guns. I had a Moto-Rumi but I sold it." But I didn't say another word. He stared through my eyes and into my boots. He did the same for Derek. He was climbing swiftly into our lives and could be about to stamp all over them and we might lose sleep over that but he wouldn't. This was his job. He was good at his job. You don't wind up as a sergeant in the Algerian army during a revolution by signing a release document at some British Embassy, or gazing at long-legged girls in Monte Carlo while drowning in a very expensive Coke. We were soft boiled eggs. He was a hobnailed boot.

"You, follow us."

We would not rightly have been described as prisoners but we had all too quickly lost our freedom of movement. In this kind of captivity you don't make decisions; they are all made for you. There is an unpleasant simplicity about such an arrangement. We did as we were told, as you do, with a gun in your face and another in the small of your back. A jeep led the way, we went after that, and a jeep brought up the rear close behind us. And the pathetic convoy drove off the road. The beige Ford Prefect sandwiched between two military jeeps. Stuff of legends! Still off the road and twenty minutes later the convoy was still moving through the landscape and nothing else coming or going in any direction. The convoy moved in no hurry at all. The soldiers had all day, and we had the rest of our lives. Derek then used the word I didn't want to hear.

"Den, we've been taken pri-so-ner."

I have no idea what was going through his mind. Perhaps it was blank like mine, like a blackboard the teacher wipes clean, but too quickly, and before you know it the questions you should have written down have been swept away and there's no one around to fill you in. It was rough country but I didn't hear the car rattling. That was probably because I wasn't hearing anything. I was staring at soldiers in a jeep, and I didn't want to look behind me. I knew the other jeep was still there. We climbed over yet another sandy rocky hill and there was a large brown building with the 'road' we were on going through the main gates, like a fort. We passed under the archway, into the main courtyard, and came to a standstill. Derek spoke again, in a voice floating on resignation, "If we come through that arch again, I hope we're still breathing." I said what I could: nothing.

We were ushered out of the car, and were told, by the barrel of a gun, that we had to stand over against a wall. Over there, white boys. And to keep our heels against the wall. So much can be said with gesture, and in circumstances like this the bare minimum - gestures have a disarming power and refuse to be contradicted, or contradicted at your extreme peril. We watched as six or seven soldiers were given detailed instructions. Standing there, heels against the wall, I slipped back into my way of life when standing at the service counter of Halfords, at the pub with Ted, on the steps of Milan Cathedral. And then I heard the action start. The soldiers at the border crossing had been almost friendly compared to what was unfolding. Without any concern at all about the integrity or the (marginal) value of our possessions, those possessions were very soon littering the ground, and in no apparent order. Basically they were ransacking the car. No, no, I tell a lie. They were taking it to bits! The rubber floor matting. Chucked out. The seats. Chucked out, rolled some distance and fell over. Boot open, bonnet up, stuff all over the place. We just watched. Do they have any idea how much care we took packing that car? How careful we have been with those seats? Do they have any idea? I was so glad that we hadn't had the idea of bringing girlfriends along for the ride. I was so glad that neither of us had thought of buying a camera. Thank heaven we didn't know anyone who had a camera we could have borrowed. Finally they exhausted themselves but had confirmed what we already knew. No camera. No guns. Sorry guys. But then we had to wait another thirty minutes while they put the car back together again, and they didn't do that the way the room cleaner tidies your bed at the Hilton. When the reassembly had been done, more gestures recommended that we leave, but not at our leisure, and we moved out through the main archway entrance and off on our travels again. Silence. We were in shock. Now at last we could breath easy. Slowly out through the arch, still breathing, and slowly back towards the road.

## *Belly up*

We found the road and we drove. Over the next 80 kms or so we were stopped and searched four times. Such repetition wears you out. We had lost so much time during that day that we decided to drive through the night. One bright idea after another. How good could it get? We had our act so tightly together and it kept falling apart, but the engine of that humble beige Ford Prefect just hummed along. What kind of scrapes we got ourselves into was up to us, but that engine was going to keep its side of the bargain and do what it had been designed to do: it would just keep humming along. It hummed. We hummed too, fitfully, more than a little shaken, and stirred too, but we hummed to that engine as we crossed the landscape in the dark.

And it was dark, black as pitch. The headlights were like feeble candles. That kept us to 50 kms an hour, at which speed the engine seemed very content indeed, the sound of silk passing through the air. We probed our way through the landscape, probed our way through to perhaps 10PM. Perhaps we would take it in turns and drive until we emerged into the dawn. But that idea was terminated by a loud bang. The car lurched sideways. The underneath of the car scraped the earth, scratched the earth loudly and definitely. The car tipped forwards. We were tipped forwards with it. The car kept moving but life stopped. The world was pitch black. We were shaken, again, but a quick check told us neither of us was hurt. At least we hadn't gone through the windscreen and suffered cuts that would have obliged us to bleed to death in the pitch black silence. Then the car pivoted to the right, and then instantly to the left and then we came to a halt. We got out cautiously - we had no idea what had hit us or what we had hit - and stepped gingerly around the car. We found a trench, some thirty metres long and a metre deep. Roadworks! No barriers around the trench, and no warning lights. After all, this was desert country and who drives through the desert at night with candles instead of powerful headlights! We had missed the trench, by good fortune, but had mounted a pile of tarmac ten metres long and half a metre high. The car was like a ship stranded on a reef at low tide.

We had been very lucky. The oil sump had not sustained any damage. The anti-roll bar and the steering gear had taken the main impact, but, unbelievably, no damage, and hitting a pile of tarmac at 50 kms an hour can do terrible damage. Thanking our lucky stars, we got the tent up and slept. Twenty four hours can make the rest of your life seem like five minutes, or less. We had taken enough for one day.

"Night, Degs."

"Night, Den. Did you remember to turn the heating off?"

You either laugh or you cry. Sometimes you do both but we were too tired to do either.

In the morning light, the car looked very odd at its angle, but routines keep life moving along. Coffee, biscuits, pack up tent, pore over the map, look down the road - and hopefully not the barrel of a gun - and make sure everything's as well as it can be. Not a trace of leaked oil anywhere. Sigh of relief. We rebuild the picture of what had happened the previous night: on the way across the tarmac obstacle we had pivoted on the rear axle. The task was now to get the ship off the reef. We emptied the boot and the inside of the car, and with the gear in neutral and the handbrake off we freed our home sweet home on wheels by lifting the back bumper and, inch by slow inch, heaving it forwards until all four wheels were touching the ground and we were back in the swim of things. As we drove along, the car pulled very very slightly to the left but otherwise it continued to hum. It hummed through Alger, and hummed all day long until, shortly before nightfall, we were close to Annababa where we would cross the Tunisian border and out of the war zone. That would be a good moment, we told ourselves, such a good moment.

We were tired of roadblocks. Our shoulders sagged: here was another one. Oh dear, not more trouble, surely. Usual procedure. About thirty men very well equipped with offensive weapons. Usual gestures: out of the car, stand there, don't move, speak when you're spoken to, and just say "yes" or "no". I thought Derek was beginning to look even older than me. There's a campfire burning and most of the soldiers are seated around it, drinking coffee and eating what looked like bread. I was hungry. The usual inspection of the car completed. One soldier came over and gestured by holding something invisible close to his face and making a clicking motion, asking that gestured question seeking to know whether or not by any chance we happened to have a camera. He certainly wasn't asking us to take his picture. And after that, we get the anticipated gesture as he lifts his gun from its holster wondering whether or not by any chance we happen to have a gun. He certainly wasn't asking us to shoot him. We shake our heads. Much to our surprise he just walked away and sat down with the others around the fire. Even more to our surprise, he turned around and smiled and indicated that we should join them. We did. Someone offered me a cigarette. Oh yes please and thank you very much, sir. Coffee? My word yes, a coffee sounds good. Milk? Two sugars? Something to eat? Have you enjoyed your time in Algeria, now free and open to visitors? Yes? Well, that makes everyone happy. And the campfire burned, and the coffee was brewed and poured and we ate bread and all was well. At last, we were welcome! It was like a party without the girls and without the music, but the coffee and the fag and the bread and the soldiers' smiles and laughter and the warmth of their campfire was sweeter than any music, though perhaps not sweeter than a girl to dance with. Even further to my surprise, a soldier leaned over and handed me his rifle, telling me, by gesture, to have a good look. I was struck by the difference between the soldier offering me his gun here around the campfire, and the soldiers not so long ago and in the same country who would have killed us rather than let us touch their guns. I lay the rifle across my lap, had a good look, and, by gesture, asked if I could try the action. He nodded: it wasn't loaded. What a change of mood, from being taken virtual prisoner and this campfire. At last, we were having really good fun, weren't we Derek! (A few years later, when I was married and ready to start a family, I had serious second thoughts about guns. A home is no place to have one gun let alone ten or fifteen of them. Maybe that moment around the campfire had been a wake-up call. By the time my first son Den was born, the guns had gone, and by the time the second son Chris arrived a year or so later, guns were none of my concern. I disposed of them legally, surrendering them to the police since at that time, conveniently, the police had declared an amnesty on guns: if you didn't have a licence you could drop them off at the local police station and not be charged with illegal possession.)

It had been another hard day's work in the desert. We asked, by gestures, whether there was any objection to our pitching our tent over there, not wanting to cramp their style at all and not wanting to drive again in the dark. Not at all, comrades, go for your life, be our guests. Our country is now free and so are you. Want to pitch your tent? Go pitch your tent, kind sirs. Make yourself at home, and sleep well. What a difference a day makes. Here we were, having feared for our lives several times, but now putting our heads on our pillows with the light from the campfire flickering through the walls of the tent, and us falling asleep to the sound of heavily armed men not treating us as a threat but effectively watching over us like parents watching over children until the danger has passed. I have fond memories of Algeria, but the scorpions had been a warning.

Near Tabarka we crossed into Tunisia and heaved a deep sigh of relief. No more being searched at gunpoint, no more check-points, just the scenery and the engine humming along. We talked more freely. Derek was convinced that if people really knew the "on the ground" circumstances in Algeria at that time, they would not believe that two young men in a beige Ford Prefect had gaily waltzed into such a war zone and emerged safely on the other side, to be farewelled around a campfire surrounded by men so well armed that they could have easily killed off everyone on Blacksmiths Lane and Francis Avenue combined. Instead, we were given coffee and bread, a couple of fags and a well-protected good night's sleep as a going-away present. Yes, I have fond memories of Algeria, and you wouldn't have to drag me back there. I knew from personal experience what being freed from oppression meant. New day, new dawn, another chance.

# CHAPTER 4:

# Egg shells

*(The Tunisian struggle for independence from France began in 1907, and continued with Habib Bourguiba. He was imprisoned, in France, in 1934, and remained in prison until 1943 when he was returned to Tunisia, after a brief transfer to prison in Italy. By 1952 the resistance had become a guerilla war and Habib Bourguiba was imprisoned again (1952-54), but this time in Tunisia. On 20 March 1956 Tunisia was declared an independent state, led by Habib Bourguiba as the country's first president, 1956-87, during which period it was relatively stable and on good terms with France.)*

### The man had said "Just go!"

Having crossed Algeria, we found out that between most North African countries there is a no man's land. Into Algeria, out of Algeria. Into Tunisia and out of Tunisia and out of Tunisia, and into Libya. We really hadn't stopped anywhere much in Tunisia, eager as we were to traverse the African continent at minimum expense and maximum speed. We headed straight for the border crossing at Gabes keen to get across and chew up the vastness of Libya. Let's go - the man had said "Just go!" So let's go! No, gentlemen, not so fast. We showed our passports. The man wasn't impressed. He wanted something else, some kind of book, a book which had a stamp in it, a stamp that proved that we had not brought anything illegal out of the country we were leaving. Oh, we realised at last, he meant that book.

Our minds went back to a small AA (Automobile Association) office, on London Road, in Stanmore, Middlesex. We remembered the man there shaking his head, telling us that we wouldn't need that book, that we should just jump in our car and go. We had jumped in our car some weeks ago, and we had just gone, like he said. And now we had come to a standstill. Without that book, this man here wasn't about to let us cross the border. I cursed. Derek looked the way Derek did when under stress: desperate, agitated. It turns out we did need that book, and we didn't have it. After several attempts to become informed, we learned that there was only one place in Tunisia where the fearless travellers in a Ford Prefect, beige to make it hard to spot in an emergency in the beige desert landscape, well, yes, that was in Tunis, the capital. I cursed, Derek cursed. We scratched our heads. "You mean, Tunis?" "Yes. Tunis. Nowhere else." "Right. Tunis. Umm, where's Tunis?"

And so there we were at the border crossing, stuck. It was around 6PM on a Sunday evening. We open up the map. Tunis is about 150 kms away. It's getting cold. After a day of 40 degrees plus, cold feels much colder than it sounds in numbers, like very cold. Not only was it cold, the petrol gauge was also telling us that we needed petrol, and this side of the border there was no petrol station. And it was 150 kms to Tunis. We had to get to Tunis or we weren't going anywhere. Tunisia is a very pleasant country, but we didn't want to stay here forever. We got in the car and closed the doors. How often had we done that already!

By the time we were halfway to Tunis, the needle on the petrol gauge had sunk further towards that letter 'E' for empty. It was resting on the 'E'. Walking down the A5 with an empty petrol can but a good chance of getting a lift to a petrol station and maybe a lift back to the abandoned car, well, that's one thing. In Tunisia and the sun gone down and the cold starting to have an effect, well, that's another thing. We just prayed. Please no. Not running out of fuel. We don't need that. We had done the right thing and gone and asked at Stanmore about that book, hadn't we? Yes. How were we to know this was going to happen? The camping carnet was the one book you just had to have or New Zealand was going to be a pipe-dream and life in Tunisia just something we would have to get used to.

Sometimes you assume one brand of bad news is about to land on you, and you fret and get downhearted, and then reality kicks in. What happens isn't what you dreaded. It's worse! We had reached the outskirts of Tunis. A miracle! Oh, Lord, thank you. What a relief. We both hear a gun shot. Shit. What was that? The car veers off the road. A puncture! Bang head on steering wheel. Ah, shit, shit, shit! Walking down the A5 with a petrol can is one thing. Walking down the road in Tunis with an empty petrol can is another. Rolling a flat tyre along the road in Tunis is quite another, at 8PM on a cold Sunday evening, and nowhere to stay the night. At least we hadn't run out of petrol and had a blow-out at the same time! That would have been good! So there we were: sitting ducks if anyone felt like shooting a duck or two.

## *Holding hands*

We locked the car and walked, looking for somewhere we could get the tyre repaired. We came across quite a few road side mechanics' places, nothing very organised, but every kind of repair work was apparently catered for. Roadside panel beating, cars in various states of decomposition, engines being rebuilt, cars without doors, missing windows, whatever you needed really, but forget about guarantees and original parts. So that was one problem almost solved. Getting a puncture repaired would not be so hard. Time to eat. It was late. We were hungry.

We found a café. A good cheap café - we had to make ends meet. We ordered, fairly much at random - we couldn't read the menu. Turns out we were due some fried goat's meat, salad and a coke. Not quite sheep's head soup but food anyway. It actually tasted quite good since we hadn't eaten meat for a while. Filling up we had cheered up too, talking merrily about how life would be with the petrol tank full again, the tyre repaired, that book in our possession. Life was sweet. It wasn't the end of the world. Yet. Not that a life in Tunisia was starting to look appealing. Just that we felt better, as you do, with at least one of three problems almost solved, and food in the stomach as well. Big stretch, and tap the stomach. "Degs, how was the food? Don't get to eat fried goat's meat everyday, do we." Big laugh. Sip of coke.

There were two other chaps in the café. Arabs, as you might expect. They had been listening to us, and understood English, and said hello and told us they had been to university in England. (How come they had and we hadn't! Seemed kind of back to front somehow. All I had to show for my education was a certificate in Metalwork and English Literature.) They offered to show us around. Why not? Guided tour of Tunis and a full stomach. Might round out the day nicely.

They lead us around the back streets. Large open windows and very large ladies of the Tunisian night. Large smiles and large everything and big desire. But no time and no money. Pity about that. We had somehow formed two pairs. Derek was in front with one of the chaps, and I followed along behind with the other chap. Holy crap! What was going on: he was holding my hand! Discreetly, trying hard not to panic and cause alarm, I slowly freed my hand, slowly caught up with the other chap and Derek, and held Derek's hand instead, if nothing else to make myself feel secure - Derek held no attraction for me - and demonstrate, discreetly, that me and Derek were fine as we were, thank you very much. But another surprise came along.

One of the fellows hailed a taxi, a Fiat 500, and then another. He got in one with Derek and I found myself in the other, with the second of our tour guides. I remembered mum telling me to never get in a car with a stranger. Well, here I was, in a car with a stranger. Once in a car with a stranger, it's the stranger who decides what happens next. What about the petrol, the puncture and the camping carnet? What about Derek? You'll go far, Logan, with that certificate in Metalwork and English Literature and a sense of adventure.

It didn't seem to take long before both taxis pulled up. Of course I had no idea where we were or how we had got there but we were somewhere, outside a bungalow set back about fifteen metres from the road. It was surrounded by a two metre high iron fence. The garden was full of date palms. We got out of the taxis and followed our hosts down the path to the large front door. They went in. It looked sparsely furnished, and I had an empty feeling in the pit of my stomach. But quite soon they appeared again, carrying a mattress each and some bedding. They put the mattresses outside the front door, on the veranda. We got the picture: we were going to sleep outside. They reminded us to take off our shoes, watched us while we did that, said goodnight, went back in and shut the door.

As I lay there, I started asking myself questions. Were they 'gay'? Were they 'straight'? Had they finished 'showing us around'? Was it safe to go to sleep? Sleep didn't seem to be on the agenda. Lost in a state of wonder and feeling rather too uneasy, I then noticed that there were two armed guards patrolling the perimeter, one coming from the left and one from the right, to cross each other at the end of the drive and carry on around the fence until they appeared again. I paid closer attention. There was a gap of about 40 seconds between when one guard passed and then the other.

"Degs, have you noticed the guards? They're armed."

"Yes. It doesn't look good. Perhaps we've fallen into a trap."

"Best we get out of here quick. Next time the first guard passes, we're going to grab our shoes, run down the drive, out the gate and off, running, and don't stop running until we know there's no one behind us."

"OK."

The first guard passes. I nudge Derek. We grab our shoes and run as quietly as we can. We kept running, paying no attention to the direction we were taking. Left, right, straight on, it made no difference to us. And then, slightly winded, we stopped, panting. We look behind us. Not a sound. We look at each other. OK, now what? It's Sunday. Derek checks his watch. 11:30PM. We're somewhere in Tunis. It's cold. People are still milling around here and there, the cafes are busy. The ladies are still smiling. Where's the car? How did we get here? We had no idea but we couldn't just stand there waiting for a miracle.

For some silly reason we started running again. We ran around a corner, which was just another corner, and could have been any corner. It wasn't just any corner. We come to a sudden stop. We are stunned. Unbelievable. Derek mutters, "I don't believe it." My eyes had probably lit up like searchlights. Our car! Our beautiful car! Right in front of us: one beige Ford Prefect, English number plate as clear as day, LXD-521. I asked myself, "Is this just luck?" We quickly got into the car, let out a long celebration shriek apiece and drove out into the desert again. We camped there, having forgotten that we were low on petrol. We slept safely. A safe exhausted sleep.

## *Pitching camp in the sea*

The next day was a Monday, fortunately. We found the office in Tunis. And, hallelujah, it was open. We bought the holy grail of that Camping Carnet, which cost us another £4 of our dwindling cash reserves. We had mixed feelings about that. Not so much about the money draining away either. The Carnet book was quite a large book, not so thick, with cardboard covers, like a ledger. All the pages are perforated. At each border crossing we should have shown it, had the list of what we were bringing into the country verified, had it stamped on both parts of the page, and watched the Customs official tear of his copy and give the Carnet back. Outside the office we each had a thumb through the book. Then Derek turned it over and checked what it said on the back. Printed there was a list of all the places in England where the fearless traveller could obtain a Camping Carnet. His finger moved down the list, and stopped.

"Hey, Den. You remember we went to that AA office in Stanmore."

I nod.

"Look, here's the address."

And there was the address: Automobile Association, London Road, Stanmore, Middlesex. We'd been there.

"Well, I'll be! And he told us 'Just go'. If we'd had that Carnet yesterday we wouldn't have been in trouble last night."

"We wouldn't have seen Tunis."

"And maybe no puncture."

"And no fried goat."

"Live and learn, hey."

We were philosophical, but underneath bloody annoyed.

After filling up with petrol, and getting the puncture repaired, we set off towards the border at Gabes once again. And then we got sidetracked. Sousse was a very seductive town, right on the coast. White buildings against the blue Mediterranean sea, beautiful place, as we would find out the next morning. Looking at the distance we had to cover we calculated the cost in fuel, the cost of bare essential nourishment to keep us alive, and came to the bleak conclusion that we did not have the necessary funds to get where we had to go. The chances of finding work in North Africa were zero.

"There's only one thing we can do: sell, sell, sell."

There wasn't a great deal to sell anyway, but we'd at least get something for a radio. Wouldn't we? Maybe. You never know your luck. But first of all, a night's sleep. It was already late and dark.

We had become quite used to camping on sand. So we spotted a tempting stretch of nice sand. "Nice and flat," I said to Derek. "Yes," he replied. "Perhaps strong persistent winds have left it flat for a change." It made sense. Usual routine. Pin down the corners of the tent, in with the poles, pin down the guy ropes, roll out the sleeping bags, and stow our valuables. Prior to lights out, we head off into the desert in opposite directions (he north-west and me south-east) to relieve ourselves at leisure, and then stretch, creep into the tent, slide into the sleeping bags, and it was good night from him. We slept extremely well. A good while after daybreak I turned over and that woke me up. Not so much the turning over as the surprise that I felt as I had done in the Lake District in my new woollen swimming trunks: saturated and fit only to be wrung out. My exclamation woke Derek up, who likewise felt wetter than wet. We were afloat! But strangely the water flowed in, and then flowed out. We opened the tent flap. We saw the Mediterranean, all around us, a lovely blue colour and the back drop of the lip of the beach and behind that white buildings.

The beach we had mistaken for desert (after all, desert is sand is sand, and then some more sand) had a very gentle slope on it, a very gentle slope. The tide had taken its time coming in. A very definite plus about this part of the world is that if you get wet (nearly always a pleasure) it is only a few minutes before you are very very dry again. We hauled everything back up the beach, spread it all out and waited for the drying cycle to finish. Not much spin but plenty of dry. In no time at all, everything is happily in the usual dry state, and we head back into Sousse to open our market to the general public. The roads were lined with date-palms and the minimal traffic included some goats and camels and the odd stray dogs, all of them looking decidedly healthy despite not getting their daily bowl full of *Pedigree Chum*. We pulled up where people were thronging and set up shop, our variety store, with the bonnet and windscreen of the car becoming our shop counter. Shirts, spare t-shirts, beaded Indian belt, guitar, plimsoles, radio. It was market stall, variety shop and curiosity shop all rolled into one. People are naturally curious. If you stop in the sunshine, by a lovely beach in a beautiful town, and spread everything you own all over your car, people take note, and put two and two together. Soon we had quite a few potential customers unable to resist their curiosity. At Halfords I had learned how to court the customer without any kind of pressure at all: just ask the question, listen to the answer, and help the customer arrive at where the customer feels inclined to go, and, above all, take a sincere interest without 'pushing'. And we let the sale begin.

Young, old, men, women, children. This way, roll up, roll up. We gestured, we held up a t-shirt, suggested to this one that, yes, you'd look good in this, and so on. We made sales, holding back the 'offer accepted' smile until it was clear that if we held back any more the sale would 'die'. We collected the cash (dinars), but turned down a few offers of barter. One customer took a keen interest in the guitar. He was dressed very 'western' in t-shirt and jeans but wasn't 'white'. He could play the guitar and tuned it; it sounded good, I told him. He looked happy. He lifted his eyebrows saying "How much?" and I lift my shoulders and spread my hands a little saying "What's it worth to you, sir?" He made me an offer, 10 dinars. I look at him, unconvinced, but not too unconvinced. He thought about it, strummed the guitar a little more, looked down the fret to make sure it was straight, tapped the back to listen for small cracks in the construction. And then he thought some more. (Never hurry a customer, even when it's closing time. They may not buy today, but treat them well and tomorrow they could be back.) I wanted to make it easy for him to spend more. Hanging from his shoulder he had a camel hair water bottle with a nicely embroidered strap. I asked if I could have a look. I liked it. I suggested, as one does when language has fallen by the wayside, I suggested that 10 dinars and the water bottle would make me a happy man. That seemed reasonable enough to him, and, under pressure, I conclude my mixture of barter and sale. At worst I could always try and sell the water bottle in a country where it might have more value. (As it turned out, I didn't sell that water bottle: it's hanging in my living room.) From time to time we set up similar stalls when cash in hand was worth more than an object on the back seat of our mobile home. We had made a reasonable amount in a short while, and packed things away, as boot sale travelling salesmen do.

Now we were really on our way. Camping carnet in hand, cash reserves replenished, and off we go, happy as you like, and before too long we're bouncing over no man's land a second time, and there's the border crossing large as life. We should have been relieved. We weren't. It was closed. Libya was closed for business. No sign of life. Not a sound. Oh, well. Nothing for it but drive a few hundred metres away and set up camp and count our blessings. We hadn't fallen prey to the ladies in the windows, for better or worse. We hadn't run out of petrol. We hadn't been raped. We'd found the car, perhaps miraculously. We'd solved all the major issues, we'd got extra cash and we'd found the border crossing a second time. We'd just have to be patient, wouldn't we.

## *This spot looks good for camping*

We made camp. Pitch tent, banging the pegs in real hard to work off the frustration. The usual routine. We had it all down pat, didn't we. Out with the Gaz cooker, make tea, nibble at something or other, wander off in different directions, last pee before bedtime, crawl into the tent, good night Derek, good night Den, lights out and see you in the morning and hope you don't snore. Some things are so simple. We were back in our routine. Thank heaven for that. Who'd want to be anywhere other than in the desert on a peaceful Monday evening on the Tunisia-Libya border?

Being woken up by gunfire, real close, has an effect. Instant tension, like rigid. I woke up as if by electric shock. My stomach is tense as iron. My testicles have shot straight back up to that place from where they had dropped all those years ago. Derek is white, a ghastly white. Together we open the fly of the tent, and peer out, petrified. We see the border post. There are some twenty odd soldiers firing their weapons in the air and waving frantically. Some are drawing circles in the sand and making gestures towards us and sticking their fingers in their ears as one who knows there is going to be a very loud bang.

"Oh, f***k me dead, Den. We camped in a minefield!"

At such moments you have flash backs. The short drive back to where we pitched tent. Banging in the tent pegs (metal) with gay abandon. Bang, bang. Job done. Next one, bang, bang. The casual stroll in different directions to have a pee. The stroll back to the tent, kicking the odd stone or two. Imagining our heads on pillows of rolled up clothing. Imagining our heads mere centimetres above a land mine just itching to go off. Sometimes you don't get too long to dwell on what might have been. The soldiers weren't messing around, firing guns in the air for laughs. This wasn't the Wild West and cowboy movies. We were in considerable danger, against which losing the car, not finding petrol, being raped - all of that was minor disaster compared with being blown to pieces. We hardly dared move. Such are the after-effects of wars. Oh shit. For the first time in my life I was genuinely, totally scared. We moved around as if on egg-shells: if we broke one shell, we were scrambled history.

We do everything very slowly. The soldiers looking on were probably taking bets on which one of us went up highest. Slowly ease the tent pegs out. Slowly fold the tent up. Slowly load stuff into the car. Tip-toe. Don't breathe. Slowly get into the car. Slowly close the doors - heavy vibration can set off a land-mine. Take a deep breath. Hold it. Let it out. Key in the ignition - Derek always drives through official situations since I don't have a full licence and shouldn't be driving anyway. Engine starts. Inch forward. Thank heaven there hadn't been a wind last night because that might have found us digging the tent and the car out of the sand. Don't think about that, Den.

Slowly, but very slowly, we close the gap between life and death and the border post. The road is all covered with sand. The human body is amazing. It's still cold at this hour of the morning in the desert, the sun still waiting to do its worst, which it will do in an hour or so. We were sweating, heavily, perspiration literally running off our faces. The border crossing guard checks through the car, comes back, opens up the priceless Camping Carnet and our passports. He stamps them, heavily. I shudder with each heavy stamp. We had been so tense. He smiles at us, with that look in his eye that tells us he knows we are quite mad, beyond hope really. He tears off the receipt section, hands the Carnet back to Derek and says something which might well have been, "God help you." Well, something had helped us. If it was just luck, then we were like cats who have worked through most of the nine lives permitted. Hard to know how many lives we had left.

As we drove off I said to Derek, "If we'd had that Carnet when we got here the first time, you know, we wouldn't have camped in a minefield." Sobering thought.

And in that mood we passed from Tunisia into Libya. The next target was Tripoli. Whatever would happen next!

# CHAPTER 5:

## Lovely day for a swim

*(From 1912 to 1927, the territory of Libya was known as Italian North Africa. There were three main traditional areas, Tripolitania, Fezzan, and Cyrenaica. During World War II, Italy lost its hold and from 1943 to 1951, Tripolitania and Cyrenaica were under British administration, while the French controlled Fezzan. King Idris had been in exile in Egypt but returned to Libya in 1944. The UN Resolution of November 21, 1949, stated that Libya should become an independent state and set a deadline of January 1, 1952, with King Idris representing Libya in the subsequent UN negotiations. On December 24, 1951, Libya became a constitutional and hereditary monarchy under King Idris. The discovery of oil reserves in 1959 turned what had been one of the world's poorest nations into an extremely wealthy state in the passing of a few years. The country remained a monarchy until the coup d'état of 1969.)*

Into Libya, bound for Tripoli and Benghazi. It isn't going from A to B. That's what the plan always says: just go, from A to B. What happens between A and B is life. Libya is a very big country where anything can happen. After the shock of realising we had slept in a minefield, perhaps we could relax. Perhaps not. After about another 50 kms of now hot driving we thought we spotted yet another dust storm whipping across the sand one or two hundred metres high. We reduced speed and wound the front windscreen down, closed all the windows and waited for the storm to pass. (They were quite common and we had a routine response.)

## *The multitude*

But it wasn't a dust storm or a sand storm. Out of the moving wall of yellowish mist appeared maybe 200 Bedouin tribesmen and their families and camels, donkeys, goats, and probably everything they owned between them. Much like Derek and I and everything we owned in the car. Every man was on a camel. All the men were fully armed, with belts of bullets crossed over their chests, swords, rifles, and we didn't stand a chance.

"OK," I said to Derek. "There's only one thing we can do. Slowly get out, wait for them, and then make it clear we are glad to see them and go around shaking hands, smiling and saying hello to the kids."

He didn't seem particularly impressed. But what choice was there? When you have no reason to defend yourself and nothing to defend yourself with except a few toothbrushes and a spare tyre, signs of genuine friendship are all you've got to see you through. So we climbed out and walked towards them, smiling through our anxiety. If it went horribly wrong, at least it would be a swift death.

The vast crowd of people and animals was upon us. As planned, we quietly went around reaching up to shake hands with the men on their camels, smiled at the children, nodding and smiling briefly to all the women, and just kept going around. A man on a camel is far more imposing and has a far better view than a man on a horse, something like the difference between driving a Volkswagen Combi and a mini-van. The one with his feet on the ground also has to reach up higher to shake someone's hand. It must be a commanding position to be in, especially armed to the teeth. The meet and greet seemed to go on for a very long time, but I never once felt at risk. It was fascinating. As far as they were concerned we were just another two white lunatics who had lost their way, clearly quite beyond help, certainly with no bounty worth seizing - had they asked or demanded, we would have offered them toothbrushes. Having seen enough, one man, obviously the chief, said something in Arabic, and everyone lost interest and the group headed off. We waved, as did a few of the children who kept looking back. And then they disappeared across the horizon, hidden from view by their own sand-and-dust cloud close on their heels but getting smaller and smaller. We were alone again, and relieved. Having only a willing friendship to give is the surest protection. Derek still wasn't completely convinced.

Back in the car, we wound the front window up again, opened all the side windows, even though it was insufferably hot, and off we went.

## *The toothbrush*

Some distance along the way across Libya, the sun rising menacingly, determined to do its worst with us again, I looked out from our tent, towards the horizon - there was horizon everywhere and nothing to see except landscape. But then I noticed a figure, an Arab tilling the earth or the sand or the rocks. He had a single camel and was following it, an old man. Perhaps he was ploughing, an old man, hunched, working to keep the share in the earth and straight. The image did something to me. There was nothing else moving on the landscape except this one figure, and the camel. It was perhaps the end of the universe and there was just him and Derek and me left, and the camel. I had never touched a camel pulling a single share wooden plough. The idea got hold of me: what would it feel like to wander along behind a camel in this wilderness, and maybe plough an area of the earth I would never see again? I would never get another chance to do this. But I had to take a gift. I rummaged through the car and all I could find that seemed like a good idea was a brand new toothbrush, from Woolworths and still in the original cellophane packaging. I showed Derek.

"A toothbrush? What's a desert farmer going to do with a toothbrush?"

"It's a gesture. It's obviously new, and perhaps useful, and it's not a pistol."

"It'll either amuse him or he'll take it as an insult. Camels have got big teeth, haven't they?"

Derek laughed and watched me on my way. After about five minutes I get close to the Arab ploughman, the camel and the single share wooden plough, but not too close. Not sure of what reception I would get, I stop, mainly because he turned around. I raise my hand, and make as broad a smile as I can. I approach him, and offer my gift - I was clearly not one of the three wise men. Since he looked a little bemused, I demonstrate that it is for cleaning teeth, indicating a bright gleaming smile as the result he could anticipate. He's an old man. He smiles, a toothy smile, wipes his hand on his black tunic, smiles back to me and accepts my gift. No doubt rattling through his head were any number of ideas, foremost amongst them might have been, "Why does a white kid appear out of the blue, offer me a gift, and there's nothing else as far as a camel can walk?" I gesture at his plough, as you would if asking someone whose language you do not speak whether you might have a try at doing what they're doing. He places the wooden plough handle in my hand, and I carefully take hold of it. Camels can be mischievous. This one moved forward with intent.. My feet came off the ground. I have taken off, hanging in space like a pair of knickers on a washing line. The old man bursts into laughter. I had travelled about ten metres in no time at all and perhaps the plough hadn't even touched the ground let alone plough a furrow. That's all I wanted really, just to know what it felt like to do that. The old man got the camel and the plough back in order, and gave me another big smile. I pat him on the shoulder, and thank him, and walk back to Derek and our little tent. For just a few seconds I had been a farmer in the desert. He and I and Derek were the same: small figures in an enormous landscape. I felt I belonged. We watched for a while and then moved on. I wondered to myself how he would explain the toothbrush, all brand new in its wrapping, to his wife or his grandchildren. Would it become a family heirloom, a trophy, hung on a wall somehow, the way hunters stick up antlers?

## *Hiding behind rocks*

Africa is hot. Water evaporates - I had learned that much at school! Water then is scarce and like gold. It's not on tap, and we were close to realising that without water, we were dead. We had two canvas water bags, one hung off the external handle of each back door, which, in some odd way was like the donkey or the camel with a leather water bag slung on each side. At this point in the journey those bags were almost empty. The car drank more than we did. And without water in the car radiator, we would have to walk. Walk where? Many a time we would decide to stop during a day's drive, whenever we found shade. Often we couldn't - there wasn't any shade, no trees, no rocky outcrops steep enough to provide shade. So we pressed on. Whizzing across the desert - where it was possible to go at speed - we finally came to an area with rocks on either side, ten to twenty metres high. I said to Derek that with rocks that high maybe there'd be water here somewhere. We thrived on optimism. It was either that or get seriously depressed and what good would that do!

A few minutes further on we came towards an opening on our left, about 15 metres wide, and as we drew level I looked through and saw, some distance away, a crowd of two or three hundred nomads, tribesmen, women, children, camels.

"With that many people and animals, there has to be water there."

Derek brightened up, and slowed down. We perhaps didn't give it a thought but our arrival would not have come as a surprise to these people. They were desert-wise and would have seen the trail of dust approaching just as clearly as they would have heard the sound of the car. They would either see the trail of dust continue past where they were or they would see the trail stop wherever we stopped and then wait, expecting someone to appear before very long. The point being that we would not be taking them by surprise. In the normal course of events the occupants of one small car would not be presenting a threat to some three hundred people, many of them probably armed.

About two hundred metres past the opening, he pulled over and turned the engine off. When it is very hot, hour after hour, it is not so easy to think straight, and alone in the middle of nowhere there's no one to ask for advice. (We had only received two pieces of advice so far. One was, "Just go!" which we accepted, and the other was "I advise you not to go" which we ignored.) But we made a plan of our very own, made up of two simple points.

1. One of us had to go and get the water, and one of us had to watch over the car, our travelling household. We'd toss a coin to decide who went and who stayed, and I agreed to make the call, and Derek would flip the coin.

2. Whoever stayed with the car would wait for 30 minutes for the other to come back. After that, he would simply drive off. 300 tribes people in a bad mood could

do horrible things to one person, so why waste two! At least one of us would survive. I remembered that moment in Gibraltar when we signed our lives away. This might be the moment of truth for one of us.

We stood beside the car and Derek flipped the coin in the hot dry air. Hopefully, I called out "Heads!" "Sorry, Den. Tails. I'll wait here." He looked a little more serious than usual. We shook hands, like maybe for the last time. I had images floating through the fog of my imagination of tribesmen aiming their rifles and filling me with holes, or, waiting until I was close enough not to be able to run away, and suddenly start after me, with whoops and shrieks, cutting me down with those curved swords. I unhooked first one bag and then the other from the back doors, slinging one over each shoulder. They weren't very heavy. Derek checked his watch. "OK. I'll wait here until …. Good luck Den."

It was a tough situation, like life or death. If we couldn't find water, we would die of thirst - dying of thirst in the desert is a very real possibility, and we'd rather like to avoid that. If I didn't make it back alive, at least Derek would have a chance to find water somewhere else. Life or death. Heads or tails. I set off. We had made an agreement, and we'd abide by that. We'd developed a bond of trust, Derek and I, and without that trust we wouldn't have got this far. As I walked towards the opening we had passed, my mind was working hard. I thought of mum, dad, my brothers and sister Annette. If I didn't make it, Derek would let them know what had happened, not that he'd have much of a clue about what had happened except that I had not reappeared and was presumed dead.

I turned to my right through the opening. About three hundred metres ahead of me was this throng, a mass of colour, mostly black and brown and some white, and movement, long robes, and as I walked towards them they became less a featureless crowd than recognisably half obscured faces, men on camels, children playing around their mothers' robes, and camels, camels everywhere. I had almost reached the edge of this mass of people and just kept walking, more slowly. Everything started to go in slow motion, and I could hear my heart thumping, and the canvas water bags had become weightless. As I drew closer, the crowd silently parted to allow me through. I was close to tears, maybe relief, maybe some deep affection for people who lived this life here under this sun and moved across this harsh desert as surely as we go from our front door to work and back. The crowd just kept parting. Maybe Moses felt like this at the Red Sea! I was exhausted, mostly by tension.

They knew already why I had come - they had seen the water bags. I was sort of led to the waterhole. No one came near and no one drank water until the two water bags were brim full. No one did anything: they just watched me. I was absolutely conspicuous and absolutely vulnerable. It is hard to describe the feeling that came towards me, especially since I had felt so exposed, an easy target, tired, thirsty, one man confronted by several hundred men and women with whom I could share nothing except the water from way below the earth, which was their land, and where they were making me feel safe and welcome, almost honoured. But I was now in a different dilemma.

Derek and I had agreed that he would wait for thirty minutes. He had checked his watch before I left him at the car. I stood there seeing all these smiling faces, many of them half covered with their headdresses to keep the sand out of their mouths, and of course they had no idea what was going on inside me. How long had it been since I left the car? I didn't know. I didn't have a watch! It could have been ten minutes or ten hours. In a way I didn't want to leave; something had happened to me, being welcomed in amongst these people, so many people, families, people who just knew the desert and nothing else perhaps. I couldn't hurry because I did not want to appear undiplomatic or greedy and just grab the water and run. After all they had stood aside and waited while I got my water before they continued getting theirs. Apart from that, I couldn't hurry anyway; the water bags were extremely heavy. So I simply started greeting everyone, the explorer and the unknown peoples of Africa, thanking everyone, with a smile for the children and a stroke on the head, reaching up to take the hands of heavily armed men on their imposing camels, and kind of nodding to the women or loosely holding a hand here and there. Their skin felt different, oddly gentle for people living in this harsh terrain. I was in a dream and I didn't want to leave, much as I also didn't want Derek to leave me behind. And there I stood torn between leaving and staying. I went and lifted the water bags onto my shoulders, with a little help and a lot of smiles and a sight those children would perhaps never forget, the white man at his most feared - I must have looked very very awkward and out of context, but may be after the War they had come to realise that white people are, well, odd but not all bad. I keep nodding thanks as I walked away with the crowd closing in behind me. But I still didn't really want to go, and I still didn't want Derek to drive away without me. Three hundred metres with two water bags is a long long way, the more so if you are determined not to make a fool of yourself and trip and fall over or feel the knees just buckle under the weight or something humiliating like that. I dared not drop the water: water's like gold. To spill water in front of thirsty people is as bad as carelessly dropping a meal on the host's carpet.

Turning left after the opening in the rocks, I see Derek. What a relief! I am shaking with the strain of carrying my burden and the release of the tension. He sees me and comes running. He shakes my hand and says, "You had another three minutes and I was gone. You cut it close." I was wheezing. "Degs, I didn't have a watch!" "Oh shit." He takes one of the water bags from me and we set them down carefully by the car. As we top up the radiator, I tell him the story. "I'm glad it was you Den. I might have lost my nerve." We laughed, poured some water over our heads, had a good couple of slugs from the tin cups, and secured the water bags again to the sides of the car. We drove off into the sun, feeling safe and fortunate. We didn't say much, except from time to time Derek would mutter something like, "Shit, Den, that could have been ugly. I didn't realise you didn't have a watch", or "Can you imagine driving across all this alone?" It's a long long way across Libya in a Ford Prefect. And doing it alone would make long a whole lot longer. Travelling by camel, and in a big group, was starting to make a lot of sense.

In the maze that was Tunis we had found the car 'by accident'. Here we had found water 'by accident'. You can't plan for that. We were perhaps riding our luck.

## *Underneath the arches*

We were cruising along. No rush. The windscreen was wound up to allow for more ventilation. The temperature of the air coming through was equally as hot as the air inside. Just the movement of air is a very slight relief, and anyway with the windows all shut you suffocate. We were thirsty. In the desert under the sun, endlessly under the inescapable sun, you're thirsty. And water is precious so you conserve it: you never know, unless you do know, like the people whose life is spent in the desert, where the next drop of water is coming from. You don't look forward to the weekend. You look forward to the next waterhole. And sometimes you look forward to something else.

Even in the desert you have to take a crap, whenever the need arises, and wherever you happen to be. Brought up in a house, going to the toilet is a private affair, and there's a special place where you do such things, and toilet paper in the desert is somehow out of place. I needed to take a crap. Urgently. Why I had left it to the last moment, I don't know, but I had.

"Degs. Can you pull over. I need to take a crap."

We had just passed over what seemed to be a bridge.

Much as I sometimes had felt that I was out of place in the desert, in my shorts and skinny ribs, you see things that also look out of place, like finding a camel on Blacksmith's Lane. Now that would be odd. Likewise, what was a bridge doing here? There was the same nothing either side of it. Bridges go across something. But there was nothing to go across except more rocks and dust and stones, and, well, nothing. Of course I could have asked Derek to stop anywhere. After all, we had been driving for hours and hadn't seen a soul, the landscape like a colour-retouched moon. Nothing of interest. No one. Just space. Get out of the car, pants down, crap, rub some dust to clean up, and off we go. It would have been easy. But I did not like feeling exposed: the psychological effect of literally being caught with your pants down tells you not to be caught out in the open with your pants down. The arch or bridge was a shelter of some sort. Plus it was some shade, merciful shade. Maybe even a degree cooler than being in the car. Any slight lowering of the temperature is welcome. And it feels secure going into somewhere or under somewhere to do a serious number two. I think it was Luther who remarked something like when you are doing a crap, that is when you should feel closest to God. I was about to find out how true that is.

I climbed down. Interesting though the structure might be, I am not on an archaeological dig. I am here to do an urgent crap. I barely notice what's around me, but I do notice it is shaded, wonderfully shaded, and just marginally cooler. Marginally. One quick ridiculous check left and right to make sure there's no one watching me. I ask myself what on earth I am checking left and right. Of course there's no one here, you idiot. Get on with it before the worst happens. Pants down. Crouch. At last. Lean forward a bit. Push. Oh boy. This is going to be good. Aahhh. That's one. Wow, that feels better. I'm under an arch, so, naturally, I start singing quietly to myself, Bud Flanagan's "No matter where I stray, underneath the arches I dream my dreams away", and have a broad smile on my face as you do when doing the urgent necessary, when ..... I heard a noise that startled me. Somewhere above my head, under the arch. On the arch. The arch! I freeze.

I glance up. I couldn't help it. You do that, when you think you're alone, and suddenly there's movement, above your head. You look up. I looked up. I wished I hadn't. "Oh, dear God!" (You see, Luther was right!) Above my head was the arch. On the arch, like a moving fresco, was a population of giant lizards. "Oh shit! Oh God!" There's hundreds of them, all staring at me, squirming around to get a better view, and I'm only about two metres below them. Fat things, all of them at least as long as my arm. Adrenalin overpowers the need to crap. Flight or fight. Flight! I stand bolt upright, whip my shorts up, and clutching the unfastened shorts with one hand I run run run run. A scrambling, desperate, life or death run, up the slope, stumbling on the rocks, and out of a canon of dread into the sunshine and the heat, panting, shaking. I can't lean on the car; the metal is blistering hot. I tell Derek about what had happened as I get some water and wash myself. He's beside himself laughing. He shouts out, "Don't understand you, Den. There's all this space, and you have to find a hole full of lizards!" I was still trembling. I look around. Nothing. No one. Back in the car, I ask him. "Degs, how do creatures get that big and that fat in this kind of landscape?" He just smiled. "Maybe they were all taking a crap too and you just disturbed their privacy. How can you be so inconsiderate, Den? I mean, it's a big country. Look. You could have done it anywhere. You don't even have to bury it. The sun will fry it in double quick time." I quite liked that Bud Flanagan song, so we sang it together, but changed the words a little, like "Lizards on the arches and Denis craps away". It's good to make your own entertainment. If only we had still had that guitar!

## *Campfire*

We end the day, as usual, looking for somewhere to make camp. The goal of getting to New Zealand was not front of mind. Having a good crap and camping in a safe place were very front of mind. Those little daily details. You might think that with so much desert to choose from, where you pitch a tent doesn't matter. We knew from our border crossing mine-field experience that it does matter, just as it does matter where you choose to have a crap. The little details so easy to overlook when you don't know what little details you are best advised to be looking for. We imagined we were getting more desert-wise by the day. Nice idea white boy. Nice idea.

As can happen, we came to a water buffalo hole. Water. Not clean water, but water. Close by were some mud huts and, looking very out of place and shoddy, structures made out of crushed 50 gallon oil drums, left-overs from the war. I'd rather live in the mud hut. Tin structures in the desert? Way too hot. We knew that much from being in the car hours on end. At night the tin hut might be warmer, but the night is well shorter than the day. We put up our tent at a respectable distance, close but not too close. After all, who would want strangers camping on their front lawn? As we're getting settled, a handful of heavily armed men casually walked across to us. Being the first to hold out a hand to shake breaks the ice. We shake hands with all of them, saying "Hello, pleased to meet you" as if they would understand. People do understand, not necessarily the language but the intention and feeling in the words. They gestured for us to follow them. We did. If you are led somewhere by a group of local men, they are probably taking you to meet someone more important than they are. I felt safer here than I had with an audience of lizards. "Trust your instincts, Den. Trust your instincts." As I've mentioned, the heads and faces are usually all covered, except for the eyes. (If you have ever had sand in your mouth or your ears or your eyes, you'll appreciate why they do that.) But what this does is force you to look carefully into the eyes - there's nothing else to look at except folds of black or very dark blue cloth. It's quite challenging, and with your full face exposed, you feel at a disadvantage, almost rude. Respect and politeness are oil on troubled waters, and can be the difference between life and death. We were learning a lot about that difference, having been right on the very knife-edge of it already, several times.

They lead us to the largest hut in the compound or settlement - the word 'village' doesn't fit. Obviously this was the main building, or the headman's home. The rest of the population had followed along behind us. It was like an adventure film. Once everyone was settled in a crowded circle, we were served tea. There were about twenty of us, very close together, seated cross-legged on the earth floor. One of the younger men could speak some English and so we slowly explained what we were doing there and what our plans were, and he translated as we took sips of this very strong tea. They all seemed happy enough with what we had said and so I gestured that we needed to get some sleep. The headman picked out four guards and gave them their instructions. They lead us out of the hut and escorted us quietly to our tent where they lit a campfire for us.

Derek was still only 25, but he had lost most of his hair, except at the sides. He looked not unlike Bobby Charlton, the football player, and both of them had the habit of combing the hair that was on the sides in towards the middle. Bearing in mind that we were near a buffalo waterhole, mosquitoes were abundant - the fire and the light having little of a deterrent effect. For our four friends, with their heads mostly covered, the mosquitoes had nowhere to feed on, but with his bald head and pale skin, Derek, to the mosquitoes, was sticking out like a sore thumb. He was being eaten alive and finally had to retreat into the tent, making sure the zip was securely closed. His head looked like a doughnut speckled with hundreds and thousands. I stayed around the fire with the four guards, occasionally bumming a fag - our budget saw cigarettes drop off the shopping list. (For better or worse, I still smoke, and when I do smoke on a summer evening, that picture of the group of us around that very small campfire in the great expanse that is Libya often comes to mind.) They gave me a WW2 bolt action 303 rifle to hold across my lap. Pretty picture in the light of the camp fire and another reminder of the collection I still had stashed away at home. By four in the morning I couldn't keep my eyes open and excused myself from their company. The sound of their voices put me to sleep. The four of them stood or sat on guard all night long and were there in the morning to make sure we got on our way after we had shared some more tea with the people and said farewell to the headman and thanked him.

## Corned beef

Two bread rolls was all the food we had left. We shared one on the way to and through Tripoli, and, with a few sips of water, that was like a small feast. We were still on the coast road between Tripoli (Tarabulus or Trables) and Misourata (Misratah), two of the main cities in Libya (Benghazi is the other one). We agreed to sacrifice another bread roll, which tasted like more of a feast than the earlier one. Getting enough to eat had become an issue. We trusted tomorrow. But we didn't need to. Out of the distance about half a mile ahead, we saw a vehicle coming our way. As it got nearer it slowed down, so we slowed down too, until both vehicles were on either side of the road. Two young Americans. They asked where we were going.

"New Zealand."

"What? This is Africa! You've got a long way to go, man."

"Hey, man, you can't go any further than that without an ice breaker!"

They both had a good laugh. Obviously going to New Zealand via North Africa was funny, especially in a Ford Prefect with canvas bags hanging off each side. They were going to Marrakech. It was the early 60s.

"Anything you need?"

"Yes. Wouldn't mind your jeep for a start! But, seriously, yes, our cupboards are bare. Everything's off the menu. We've eaten ourselves out of house and home."

We went over to their very well-appointed all-terrain jeep, almost like a small mobile home and air-conditioning too, and they pulled out a 2.5 kg tin of corned beef.

"You sure?"

"Wouldn't give it to you otherwise, man. Enjoy. We've got plenty."

"Great. Thanks. This is like a Christmas dinner!"

They got back in and drove off, waving through the windows. Then the arms disappeared inside, and no doubt the windows went up and no doubt the air-conditioning went back on. I looked at their jeep. They had four professional looking water containers on the back. The jeep was nicely high off the road surface. I looked at our Ford Prefect, kind of low slung like an old mattress, and the canvas water bags hanging off the sides. Oh well. Some people travel in barges, and some people travel in yachts. OK, so ours was a barge. I could live with that. I didn't have a choice: it was Derek's anyway. Americans were so confident. But they were driving into the sun. At least we were driving away from the sun. That made me feel better. (But having a good look inside that very well-appointed jeep had made a deeper impression on me than

I realised at the time. Well-appointed vehicles would later become a significant part of my life.)

And there we were, sitting in the front of the Ford Prefect with a 2.5 kg tin of corned beef. Unbelievable. Only a few minutes before the Americans' arrival we had eaten the last of the last bread roll. Let's get into it! Derek gave me the tin.

"Here. Hold this in between the seats."

He found a couple of spoons, took out the jack-knife that was always hanging from his belt, and, while I held on tight, he cut around the lid, and then bent it back.

"Look at that, Den! Just look at that! Food! Tuck in."

We tucked in, recklessly, mouthful after hasty, greedy mouthful, until half the tin was empty, until we couldn't get any more down our throats. Mistake number one. I got out of the car, to stretch: I was so full I could hardly walk. We then drove on until we came to yet another collection of mud huts and crushed oil drum shacks, needing something other than water to wash the corned beef down. We found a mud-floored café. They sold milk by the glass. We had a glass of milk each, and drank it fast, too fast. Big gulps. Mistake number two. We were now bloated, almost inflated. It hurt. On reflection, we had been better off hungry! They sold cigarettes as well. How I would have loved a cigarette, but beggars can't be choosers, and reluctantly I looked away. Anyway, I consoled myself, smoking probably wasn't doing my ulcers any favours.

## *Anyone for a haircut?*

Many a time we had looked at our much-folded map of North Africa to see where we were headed. We were not led on by tourist attractions or beauty spots - we had no idea where they were! What led us onwards was not that, and not New Zealand: it was the basic hunt for the essentials of water, fuel, food, and in that order. We had never thought of a haircut as being a reason to go somewhere next. This applied to our next choice of stopping place, Buerat, or somewhere very near there.

While not exactly packed with precision, all our belongings are in the back of the car. It's a very bumpy stretch of 'road', sand, rocks, mud, dust, and getting worse by the minute. Derek should have slowed down, like we shouldn't have camped on a minefield. And then we did slow down. No. We stopped dead. Everything in the back jumped into the front like over-excited children. In a flash, I was wearing a suitcase on my head, and the other one hit Derek in the back of his. We'd hit a rock, but no damage done. Having stopped all of a sudden, we decided we would have a look around: the stop must have been 'meant'. As happens round here, there were a couple of huts. And as also happens, one was a barber's shop that sold cigarettes, and the other establishment sold coke in bottles and petrol in large tin cans. An odd pairing of demands needing a source of supply, but there we were. Obviously I needed a hair-cut. My hair was getting long and I didn't like it long. It was also a long time since I had felt the luxury of having my hair cut. I had suffered enough. No wonder Derek had stopped dead. Instinctively he just knew what I needed. I sat in the wooden chair, and the man cut my hair. So far so good. Obviously I would have to pay. Umm. How much? Right. I didn't have any money in any currency that was worth anything in this particular hut somewhere in Libya. Derek and I had that much in common. The guy is standing there. I indicate: Me (pointing at my chest) go to car (pointing to car) and fetch (indicating pocket) uh...fetch something. I point again to the car and then to the spot where we are standing, which is my guarantee that I will come back and meet my obligations. I return with my Burton's suit. Do not ask me why I had packed a suit to go to New Zealand through North Africa. Do not ask questions like that. I had. And some things you do just on instinct, like Derek stopping dead. The barber looks at it, and taps his pocket and lifts his shoulders with a question, asking me if I have cash. I shake my head and point to the suit.

Negotiations were underway. I had never had to negotiate before, not to pay a barber. I had never imagined that my first test-run at negotiating would be for payment of a hair-cut, in a little hut somewhere in Libya. He tries it on. That suit had cost me £9/19/6 (nine pounds, nineteen shillings and sixpence), about three days wages. Well, that's not quite true. It hadn't finally cost me quite that much because I had bought it on the never-never, that installment plan that seems to go on and on and on, like roads or tracks across the desert. It still wasn't legally mine, since I hadn't yet paid it all off. But the barber was not to know that, was he. He stroked it. He liked it. Thank goodness for that. I bargained because, number one, he seemed to have decided that I would part with the suit in complete payment for the haircut. Wrong. Wrong. Wrong. I had seen the cigarettes for sale. I indicate that I would like a quantity of cigarettes added to his side of the scales of justice. I point to the cigarettes and tap my suit, indicating he should lay the cigarettes on the suit. He does. At first a sad and lonely single cigarette. I smile and shake my head, and encourage him to offer a more fair settlement. He adds another cigarette. No deal. And another. Still no deal. He adds a fourth and folds his arms across his chest. Clearly he has reached his limit. Derek has become impatient and appears at the door. Clearly I have reached my time limit. I extend my hand. He gives it a firm grip. I walk out with four cigarettes. They weigh a lot less than a Burton's suit. They also don't last as long, and do not keep you warm when you have precious else to keep you warm. If smoking is a sin, then one sin would one day lead to another. At least we had a little more space in the back of the car and less to catapult forward if we ever had to do another emergency stop for a rock.

We pressed on. Libya is a very big country. It was seeming to get bigger by the day. Perhaps the rest of the world was Libya and, magically, New Zealand would appear where Libya stopped. Perhaps not. Day after day we drove across Libya. We couldn't afford to stay anywhere so we had to camp because if we stopped anywhere, we would end up spending money. We had less and less money that we were more and more concerned about not spending. Our expedition funding had been ad-hoc. The Ovaltine biscuits were a childhood memory. The aluminium cigar tubes of Nulacyn wouldn't last much longer. The salt tablets we had jettisoned. We were up against it. The car boot sales had continued. One Burton's suit gone to the highest bidder for a haircut and four fags. Smart deal, Den. You should have brought more suits!

## *A swim in the ocean: beige on beige*

Still some 500 kms from Benghazi, we had at least gone some distance past El Agheila. Rommel and Montgomery had had a minor confrontation there about twenty years before, shortly after I was born. My birth was of course not on their minds at the time, and, at this time twenty years later, we were not thinking about Rommel or about Montgomery either: we were thinking about going swimming. The desert can do that to you. Just imagine. Close your eyes. It's a hot, hot day that has been going on forever. You have almost forgotten what shade is. You have been driving forever. Libya is going on forever. Your skin is dry and feeling dirty. A swim? Did someone say a swim? Oh, yes, please. Let's go for a swim.

It was perhaps around 9:30 in the morning. It was already hot, but not as hot as it was going to get, as surely as a man loves a woman. I looked ahead.

"Degs! Just look at that! The sea!"

I pointed through the windscreen to that deliciously refreshing blue ribbon that was the sea. We hadn't seen the sea or any expanse of water since even before Libya came into existence and neither of us knew how long ago that was. But I knew what sea looked like, and that was sea, straight ahead, there on the horizon where I'm pointing. Look!

"No, Den, you're imagining it. The sky's blue, but there's no sea."

Maybe he was right. But about a quarter of a mile further on, over another gentle hill, there it was again. It was getting closer. It was unmistakable. Even Derek could see it now.

"Well, knock me down with a feather. You're right!"

I smiled. The sea.

"Let's go for a swim, Degs."

"That sounds good to me. I'm sure we stink."

We park the car in the desert. No white lines. No "No waiting" signs. No meters. No traffic wardens. No parking tickets. Hallelujah! A swim! and all the time in the world.

We agree it's probably no more than a five-minute walk, only a little less than the Lake district was from Blacksmiths Lane. We get down to our shorts and grab a towel each. You might wonder why we bothered to take a towel when the sun would dry us off within seconds of getting out of the water. We didn't think about that any more than we thought about Rommel or Montgomery. It was a basic necessity to have a towel each. You just don't go swimming without a towel, the same as you don't take a crap out in the open desert, just in case someone is looking, from about 90 kms away. The sensible thing to do is to take a crap in the shade with heaven knows how many lizards waiting to drop onto your head. We had our towels and felt good. Now we were in our element. It was like some imaginary childhood outing we had never had. Happy days were here again. A swim! Let's go!

There is an old army saying: "Wander fifty metres from camp and you are lost." We had walked some long way past the fifty metre mark when we came to the top of a small rise. There it was again, that beautiful, unmistakable ribbon of oceanic blue, an unbelievably clean and refreshing ocean, wet and cool and longed for. We stood and gazed. The increasing heat of the sun was bearing down. That amplified the desirability of that refreshing water.

"Isn't that strange," Derek said. "From the top of that other rise I could have sworn that the ocean was just past this one. But look. It's just a little further. Can you see?"

Of course I could see. A blue ribbon of ocean. Clear as day. Bet my life on it. We got to the top of the next rise, all the time totally convinced that on the other side we would be able to throw down our towels and run and then splash and then leap into that blue refreshment of clean clean water. It happened again, and again: top of a rise, see the ocean, down a slope, up a rise, almost imagining the sound of the sea lapping against the shore on the other side, get to the next ridge, and there's no ocean there. How odd. Oh well, press on now that we've come this far.

I strode on down the next slope until I noticed that Derek wasn't keeping up with me. He had draped the towel over his bald head. His head had dropped and his chin was bumping against his chest, kind of flopping up and down as he tried to walk. It was so disappointing, getting to the top of the next rise full of hope and expectation, so ready for a swim, only to see more sand and the ocean, as if teasing us, hiding beyond the next ridge. Derek was moving more and more slowly and didn't seem to be looking where he was going, like on automatic. He wasn't saying anything. I was tempted to go on ahead and check out just the next rise, but something stopped me. I looked back. Derek was lying down. You don't lie down on the desert sand and go to sleep. The sand is too hot. We would just have to give up and retrace our steps. I looked this way, and there was that ribbon of ocean. I looked another way, and there was that ribbon of ocean. I looked another way. Same thing. We were surrounded by ocean, always no doubt just another ridge away. I accepted that we would have to retrace our steps. I looked around. Which steps? There were no tracks to be seen. Then I remembered that army saying. I tried to think. What does it mean to be lost in the desert? There aren't that many policemen hanging around waiting to field a question. If you are lost, you cannot find where you came from. Where had we come from? I didn't know. We were lost.

I got back to Derek. He sat up. That was a relief. I looked into his eyes. They were all bloodshot, like really red. I'd never seen eyes looking like that. He said he was fine, the way a drunk says he isn't drunk, it's just that he can't get up. He didn't look fine. Then I noticed there was this gummy stuff around the corners of his mouth. What did that mean? He needed water. We hadn't brought any water with us on our little walk to the beach. Who takes water to the beach? The water is what lures you on. And there I stood. Somewhere on the face of the earth. Somewhere in Libya. Some distance from any expanse of water. Somewhere in a particular spot of desert, and somewhere in a very specific spot of bother. We were in trouble, I told myself, real trouble. If I had insisted on going to the beach in spite of Derek's objections I would by now have been feeling wretched. But we had both seen the blue ribbon of ocean. That made me feel a little better, but not a whole lot. Out under the desert sun at perhaps something coming up to high noon and without water, and one of you obviously showing the effects of something not very healthy, the desert will kill you more without fail than a wandering nomad with a rifle. I kept my thoughts to myself. From what I could see, Derek was past thinking. I was right about that.

Once you take the body past a certain point of exhaustion or overheating, the process of collapse continues to the bitter end, unless an appropriate intervention is made. In the situation we were in the most essential interventions were shade and water. We had neither. For a while Derek seemed almost steady on his feet, and so did I, but then we started to lean on each other, arms around each other's shoulders. There we were: two figures in a landscape in shorts and sandals, with our towels as if we had just come back from the beach. I had a good head of hair (but why had I decided to have a hair cut!) Derek was as good as bald so the towel was his only protection. It kept slipping off his head. I'd put it back on again and he'd sometimes mutter "Thank you" and sometimes he didn't say anything. I had mine over the back of my neck and my shoulders. They weren't big beach towels, just hand towels. I knew that I had to protect my neck and make sure Derek's head was covered. That's all I could do. And if I started to wilt, there was no way Derek would be able to help me.

I started praying, seriously praying for help. The sun was grinding its way up to the middle of the sky and burning my brains out. We weren't even thinking any more, not even about where we were headed. I started to feel like crying, wanting to give up. I couldn't stop myself wanting to give up. I had forgotten that if I gave up, then Derek and I would certainly.... I couldn't even think about that. I gave up. I felt drunk. The sun wouldn't leave me in peace. I felt drunk, smiling, tired, too tired. I wanted to sleep. Just let me sleep. And I lay down and curled up in a ball, and I was looking at the Lake District, my place, where everything was safe and I had my swimming trunks that I was so proud of. Lets go there Derek. And I closed my eyes and went to sleep.

Derek woke me up. He was pulling me up. Maybe he was stronger than me, being four years older. He hauled me to my feet, and then we propped each other up and stumbled on. On. In which direction is on? What is direction? Where is where? Where you came from? Where did we come from Derek? Derek didn't know if we had come from anywhere. We weren't walking or stumbling really. We were just dragging one foot as best we could through the sand and the stones, through the sand and stones. We went forwards. You have to go forwards, even if you're going round in small and very slow circles. Forwards means something good. Backwards means it's all over. Fall over and it's all over, backwards or forwards. We had obviously come from nowhere and we were determined to get back there if it killed us. And there was no one to help us do that, so we would have to help ourselves.

"Is it further than we thought, Degs, or are we just taking too long?"

"You think?" said Derek. His eyes were shut. He was delirious.

I wasn't thinking about anything. I was absent. Derek was just heat and weight. I felt how it was to go to Communion at Catholic church as a youngster. *I was there. You were there, weren't you Den? You were eleven years old. Communion, on Sundays. It was peaceful, wasn't it Den? Den are you listening to me? It was good, wasn't it, that peaceful atmosphere, the coolness of the church, the singing, the prayers, the wafer on the tongue and I shall not want. Pray Den, pray for me. Let us pray Den.* Maybe that saved me, that brief remembrance of prayer on a Sunday because after that I felt better. We had stumbled onto the road, covered here and there with sand, but it was road. We looked up and down the road. No car. Standing beside it, road goes left or right. The sun was high so we didn't know which way might be east and which way might be west: all directions were the same. But a car might come along this road. We had agreed that we had seen the blue ribbon. We had agreed to take our towels - and thank heaven we had. Some time long ago, we had agreed about who would face the nomads and try and fill the water bags and who would stay with the car. We would now agree on which way to lurch, perhaps never to lurch again. We both felt left was to be preferred. Perhaps left went to Benghazi. We were planning to get to Benghazi. We could both remember that. We went left.

## The Lane via Benghazi

"We haven't been to Benghazi yet, have we Degs?"
"Don't remember, Den. It's nice word, Benghazi."

Both of us were covered in salt stains. We were both badly sunburned - we hadn't thought about sunburn. We were both as good as dead on our feet, but somehow or other we swayed along the road. After a period of time that might have been as big as Libya for all we cared, Derek looked up. I couldn't keep my head up but somehow he managed to look up.

"Den, car coming. Headlights on. See it, Den?"

We stopped and I struggled to lift my head up. Yes, I could see it too.

"Yes. It's a bright headlight."

"Maybe we will make it after all."

It would have been sensible to have stopped where we were and waited for the headlight to reach us, but compulsively we swayed on, going forwards, never go backwards, never give up. Not now, Den, not after coming so far. We stopped now and again. The light was only marginally closer. We swayed, dragging our feet, feeling very sick. The only thing that kept us swaying was that headlight. We stopped.

"It must be waiting for us. It doesn't seem to have moved."

The sun was starting to move towards a horizon. The light had come closer. Then, when we were about two hundred metres away, the light went out and there was nothing but sand. But we kept going forwards, very slowly, but forwards.

"If we stop, we'll fall over." I felt like crying but couldn't be bothered.

"Where's the light gone?" Derek sounded horrified.

About thirty or forty metres away, both of us recognised a shape. A car. A beige car. The sun had been shining on the small back window, and as the sun moved so the reflection was turned off. We hadn't found the car: that beautiful, precious Ford Prefect had found us. I turned and thanked the sun. It had brought us full circle.

Water. I headed for the water bag. Derek cautioned that we should just take small sips, swallow a little and then make ourselves throw up as the water might be brackish. He made himself sick; I couldn't. I got straight into the car, opened all the windows. Derek got into the driver's seat and started her up. Full of life. Nice throaty sound. He looked at me. The whites of his eyes were completely red and when he looked at me, he didn't look at me at all; it was if he wasn't behind his eyes any more; his eyes were empty. Something was definitely not right. Maybe he was dead.

The car went into gear, the handbrake was released, the accelerator was depressed, and Derek drove the car straight across the road, up the dune opposite and the car rolled onto its side. Fortunately it ended up at a mere 45 degree angle, with Derek on the upside. I managed to crawl over him and slide out through the window. Where the strength came from I do not know, but I had enough to tip the car back onto four wheels. Derek was almost unconscious. I manhandled him into the passenger seat.

## *Grand Hotel, Benghazi*

The car wouldn't start. Apart from my excellence at Metalwork (practical and theory) I had developed an interest in engines, including that of my Moto-Rumi. Often a car won't start because the petrol in the carburator has evaporated back into the petrol tank - especially in hot climates. The trick in that case is to pour petrol directly into the carburator, and turn the ignition key. Hopefully, the engine will then fire and turn over, the suction through the carburator will draw fuel up the fuel line (like water sucked up through a straw) and the engine will keep turning over as normal. That's what I had to do, and that's what I did. Hey presto, the engine started. It sounded healthier than Derek looked. There were perhaps two or three hours of daylight left to play with.

After more or less forcing two aspirin into Derek, and making sure he had absorbed some water, I drove off towards Benghazi. And I drove, for a couple of days. At night I set up the tent, dragged Derek out of the car and, with a little co-operation from him, manoeuvred him into his sleeping bag, and then gave him some more water and a biscuit or two - the corned beef was already gone. He was still very weak, although his eyes were beginning to clear and he seemed to be more in the present than he had been. I have no idea what condition I was in, except that I was capable of driving and he wasn't. During the day, I just drove, administered some water to Derek, and a biscuit, and then drove on again. My four cigarettes had also gone up in smoke. They probably helped keep me calm and suppressed my appetite. Finally we arrived on the outskirts of Benghazi. I nudged Derek.

"We're here."

"New Zealand? Already?" It was a mildly hysterical laugh, like a drunk.

Was he starting to pick up or was he about to peg out?

"No. Benghazi. You feeling any better?"

"I can see straight. What's your name, kid?"

And after a few seconds, "You got a licence to drive my car?"

Into Benghazi. Palm trees, people walking along the streets, half decent roads, a comforting world after having crossed all the time of existence in Libya. But for a nomad with a camel, seeing the desert again and no people and no palm trees might be as comforting as these streets were for me. All I thought we needed was water, as usual, and a good wash and scrub up, especially for Derek who looked still very wrecked. We both must have looked very wrecked. Salt stains, cracked lips, acute sunburn, very wonky eyes, dirty clothes, and smelling to high heaven. Clean water was on my mind so I picked on a very swish looking building, something from a movie set, and decided that's where we would ask for a little kindness. It was called *Grand Hotel*. I could imagine Humphrey Bogart staying there. You might remember *Casablanca* and the song *As time goes by*, the song that Sam played, or the line "Here's looking at you, kid". Casablanca was a long way behind us and time had certainly gone by, as it does. In front of us, *Grand Hotel*. And it looked like a grand hotel, way beyond our means, but a tempting thought - sheets, a comfortable bed, food on plates. "Yes," Derek said. "Keep on dreaming Den. Anything could happen."

I was wearing my shorts, sandals, and a shirt for modesty, and I am sun-burned to hell. Plus I have been driving for the best part of three days, sunrise to sunset. Unperturbed by how I might be seen or what anyone might think of me, I walk into the foyer of Grand Hotel. It's marble. Palm trees inside. Statues of this and that figure - I have no idea who. It's posh. It's grand. I am no Humphrey Bogart but I played my part. There was a large man at the Reception Desk. He wore, in contrast to my informal get-up, a white tuxedo, black bow tie, white shirt, and a red fez. He said he could understand English. I asked if by any chance we might be able to fill our water bags, use the toilet, wash and comb our hair and feel normal again. I didn't see him but another man had walked past me in his white safari suit, worth a good number of haircuts and quite a few fags, I dare say. He must have heard me talking.

"Excuse me, sir," he said as he came back towards Reception, "are you English? Where's your tourist bus?"

"There is no tourist bus, sir," I replied. "There's just me - I'm Den - and my friend Derek who's out in the car with severe sunstroke. The car's out on the street, a Ford Prefect, beige. We've driven from England, down through Gibraltar and across North Africa to here. But we're not stopping. We're on our way to New Zealand."

"Say no more. My name's Ken." We shook hands. He gave me a very serious look. "Stay exactly where you are. Don't move. I'll be back." What had I done wrong?

And he disappeared through some glass doors into what looked like a large dining area. I just stood there, not a little confused. The man in the fez just smiled and said I looked tired. I felt rather conspicuous. I don't like feeling conspicuous, but the atmosphere was a tonic. The glass doors opened again and Ken appeared followed by perhaps a dozen other men, all very well dressed.

He whispered to me, "What's your friend's name?" and I whispered back, "Derek", as if we were sharing some very private secret. He waited until they had all found a space around me, with Ken standing next to me. "What you are looking at, gentlemen, is one young man who has driven from England with his mate, Derek, in that...." and he pointed across the road to where the Ford Prefect was leaning in rather weary fashion against the kerb. Everyone broke into applause. "OK. Den. You go and fetch Derek in, and dinner is on me. There aren't so many young chaps who drive to Benghazi via Gibraltar."

I was taken aback by the enthusiasm of the reception. It was like recognition that we had made a remarkable journey. We knew we had. Clearly Ken knew we had as well. But I was back out in the hot street, easing Derek out of the car and supporting him through the foyer and into the restaurant. As we tottered in, everyone in there stood up and applauded us again and cheered. My eyes were brim full. Three days earlier we had been as good as dead, and now this to welcome us back to the land of the living. It was like a dream. How come I picked out this hotel? How come Ken happened to overhear what I said? How come we hadn't died? As I said, my eyes were brim full.

Seeing what was before those eyes of mine, perhaps we had died. Perhaps we were in paradise getting our just rewards for shaking a lot of hands and smiling when in doubt. Great big tables covered in starched table-cloths. Silver cutlery, like substantial silver cutlery. Bottles of Chianti in their straw containers. Baskets of bread, of fruit. We had roast chicken, roast potatoes, vegetables, and then dessert and coffee afterwards. And there at the table, in his white safari suit, our saviour, Mr. Ken with whom we were sharing some of our exploits and near misses. Ken worked for BP, as did all the other men, his staff. He was on £4000 a year, around 4 times the £1000 that most people dreamed of. He was all ears as we explained our plan to drive to Alexandria, through Israel, and then turn south towards Yemen or through the Suez canal and from there somehow to New Zealand.

"You've got a long long way to go yet, my friends, but for now you're staying right here at *Grand Hotel*. A few days rest and recovery, see Derek is back in good shape, feed up a bit... stuff like that. It'll do you good. You've taken a bashing out there. Best take a break from the road. Don't worry about the cost. For the guys, it's inspirational. They complain too easily. You guys are extraordinary. An amazing tale. And you haven't finished yet! You're not even half way." About himself he was very modest.

Until that night I had no concept at all for a 'luxury' hotel. Not on my map. Way beyond my reach. And yet, not reaching for it, there it was, right in our laps. Two single beds, crisp cotton sheets, bedside table, ornate bedside lamps, thick carpets, shower and bath, soap, enormous towels and a panoramic view. Amazing. While we were there I found the hotel letterhead paper and wrote my only letter back home, to my brothers and sister and dad. I still have it. It is the only letter I wrote while we were on our way to New Zealand. Before we left the hotel, Ken arranged to have two new tyres fitted for us, at his expense (or BP's), and as if that wasn't enough he filled our petrol tank until not another drop would fit in. Derek was back on his feet, his eyes had cleared, and we had been extremely well fed and watered. The contrast between actually believing we were shortly to die in the desert, hopelessly lost, barely able to stand up, not wanting to stand up, and the complete opposite we had arrived in at *Grand Hotel*, Benghazi, with the food and wine and sheets and good company. Of course we thanked Ken before we left. But how could we possibly thank a man like Ken for what he did for us? Hard to say. Perhaps, one day, just by doing the same kind of thing for someone else who needs help getting back on their feet.

## *Saying thank you*

Going towards Egypt the coast road from Benghazi passes through Albayda, Dema and then Tubruq (Tobruk). It's a small place, but famous and one of the few places in North Africa that I had seen pictures of, in newspapers. There were a lot of people, living close together, many in shacks made of more 50 gallon oil drums crushed flat and somehow fixed together to make a shelter. The drums were left-overs from the second World War, and, on the positive side, at least some good use was being made of them in peace time. We knew a little of the history of Tobruk and knew about the War Graves. With the mood of war recently in our faces, we went there, to Tobruk War Cemetery.

We had really forgotten what grass looked and felt like, and it was the well-watered green grass that made the first impression. It was so green and it would have been tempting to just lie down on it, but there is a mood about this cemetery which affected us immediately. Some buildings have an atmosphere which has an instant impact, a sense of wonder that slows you down and you feel still and forget the rest of the world as if suspended in time. Walking through the massive arch at Tobruk has that effect, even with the khaki anti-aircraft guns either side of the entrance. For me, the place felt sacred. We didn't speak. The green lawns were all neatly mown and the edges trimmed and against this fresh green stood the precise rows of white headstones as far as the eye could see. So much white, so crisp. I was conscious of the white of Ken's safari suit and the white of the cliffs of Dover, but that fades away and what strikes me is the contrast, between the circumstances in which these people died - noise, chaos, losing friends before they too are stopped in their tracks - and the neatness, the order, the serenity of this space. As an expression of gratitude it made sense: it was so appropriate that those who had died in those circumstances would be remembered, even namelessly, in this space of calm and reflection. It was oddly beautiful and emotional. I am sure both Derek and I reflected on how fortunate we had been in Algeria. The fact was that we had been fortunate wherever we had been.

We walked away and back to the car. We were content not to speak and the car hummed peacefully along as we drew close to our next port of call, Alexandria. But before that happened we had the Libyan-Egyptian border to cross.

# CHAPTER 6:

# On top of my world

*(Britain and France had been the dominant colonial forces in modern Egypt, and a kingdom until 1954 when King Farouk was deposed in a military coup. On June 18, 1953, the Egyptian Republic was declared, and in 1956 Gamel Abdul Nasser, the major driving force in the 1952 Revolution, became Egypt's first President. In July 1956, he nationalised the Suez Canal (built by French engineers), which until then had been open to international shipping as the canal was deemed to be international waters. That act sparked the 'Suez War' of 1956. After the 'war', the Suez Canal was fully under Egyptian control, and by 24 April 1957 also fully opened to shipping.)*

We crossed the Egyptian border at Umm Sa'ad. Again that question came up, "Where are you going?" We were tired and once again not eating well. The man at the border post asked again.

"Our plan is to cross Egypt, pass through Israel and then on towards New Zealand." And Derek nodded.

"If you come into Egypt, you will not be able to enter Israel, and if you want to go anywhere after Egypt you will have to go by sea."

We already had thoughts in our heads, of Beirut, Damascus, Iraq and whatever came after that. But those thoughts were about to be chipped out of our thinking and thrown into the rejected goods bin with a resounding clang. Derek rarely showed any emotion, but I could see the water welling up in his eyes. We had travelled across so many thousands of kilometres, had come close to death, had survived some very close escapes from one kind of danger or another, and all that just to be turned back at the very point where we just wanted to turn off and head south! It was unthinkable, completely unacceptable. No, we said, no, that is not on our agenda. But the man was unmovable. What could he do to change the history of this part of the world? Only five or six years before there had been a war here too, over the Suez Canal, between Egypt and Israel and between Egypt and France-Britain as well. The Egyptians, under Nasser, had fought their way to an independence from both Britain and France but Egypt and Israel would continue to be on very edgy terms with each other as everyone knows. We couldn't go backwards and we couldn't go forwards as we had intended. All other options had been shut down. Sympathetically, the official stamped our passports and disconsolately we put them in our pockets and thanked him. He could see that we were gutted. But we had hit the brick wall of the state of the world, smack, like a fat insect through the windscreen, and we slid down that wall in a heap.

In the courtyard outside we sat on the ground and stared between our knees. We sat there for a long time, occasionally fighting back the tears, taking deep breaths, staring up at the sky, staring down between our knees, fighting back the tears manfully. Stumped. Den and Derek, check mated. State of the world 10 - Den and Derek 0. No extra time, no replay and no point complaining. We were stumped. It was very odd. In the desert we had come as close to death as you can without actually dying, and yet we had not felt stumped, not like this. But told we could not go through Israel, and we felt stumped. The desert experience was somehow natural: this one was brutal. Accepting death had not been hard, so this door closing on our fingers should not be hard to accept either. But it was and it took some time to come to terms with the reality. If this scene was in a movie, it might show the border official outside the building, having a cigarette and looking across towards us, seeing our heads slumped. Perhaps such a scene would create the impression, through his body language and the look on his face, that he felt sympathy for us, or at least empathy. The reality was more likely that he just got on with whatever he had to be doing, wondering at the same time what on earth white people had inside their tiny little minds, wondering how on earth two young men, who could easily have been fighting on the banks of the Suez Canal had they been born just two or three years earlier than they had been, how could two such young men be so naïve! Didn't they read newspapers? Had no one told them?

We started talking.
"Well, Degs, what's Plan B?"

"I don't really want to think about it but I guess we have to. We could see if we can get on a boat that will go through the Canal and then down to New Zealand that way."

We thought about that.

"Or we could go from Egypt to Cyprus and see where we go from there."

It seemed like the less stressful of the two options, and we settled on that. We were not feeling very strong, not so intrepid as we had been.

"OK. We're in Egypt. Might as well get to Alexandria, since that's what we told everyone we would do."

"Right. Alexandria."

We shook hands on it. Neither of us looked very bright. The truth is we would have preferred to stay there, sitting and staring at the ground.

Not far out of town and short on petrol yet again. We had been filling the tank and filling two or three cans with petrol as a stand-by. We were down to one can, again. Spotting an old and battered single pump by the side of the road, we pulled in. The pump had those twin glass bowls at the top of the fuel hose, to indicate that petrol was flowing. An old man came out in a turban, baggy trousers and three quarter length Arabic tunic. We gestured that we needed to fill up and he promptly disappeared around the back of a shed. The silence was broken by the sound of a 4-stroke engine coughing into action. The bubble thing at the top of the fuel pipe bounced around and the old man reappeared and filled the tank for us and the empty cans as well. We settled up with him - he picked out what he needed from Derek's hand, and we had to trust him because we were new boys on the block and had no idea what to give him. And off we went.

## *Dear Cliff, we're on our summer holiday ....*

By now we had sold pretty much all our belongings except the clothes we wore and the essentials like the tent and sleeping bags and the Gaz cooker. As the car emptied, so the payload diminished, and as the payload diminished so we were probably achieving a more efficient fuel consumption - the engine only had me and Derek left to carry. So there was a bright side: we had less but could go further, until of course we had absolutely nothing, but by then perhaps we would be under the long white cloud with our feet up reading letters from 'back home' and listening to sheep bleating through the kitchen window of a neat little homestead.

Alexandria was by the ocean so we wouldn't have to worry about water for a while. It was a busy seaport, and seeing the ships and recognising that we had finally at least reached Egypt picked our spirits up. Never mind what we couldn't do, we thought, let's just concentrate on what we can do. Getting this far had been a miracle of sorts, and it would be ungrateful to spoil that achievement by not making the most of where we had arrived. We settled on driving down through Cairo, through the agricultural area and, if we did nothing else in Egypt, we would at least see the pyramids. And that was how we found our energy levels filling up again.

The following day we headed for El Giza, Cairo and then through the agricultural landscape. After what we had passed through on the way there, what we saw was something incredible, almost shocking. It was all so amazingly green, acres of green date palms, cultivated fields stretching away, stuff growing in profusion. This part of Egypt anyway looked like an enormous oasis to get to which you had to cross an eternity of barren lands, with brief relief here and there almost begrudging. Just seeing more colours was healing for the eyes. Contradictions all over the world.

Since our time there out on the road, package holidays have become as common as toothpaste. The wonder of Egypt has been circulated in millions of tourist brochures and on many millions of digital cameras and on thousands of sites on the Internet. But in 1962, even holidays in Spain or Italy or Sardinia were only just starting to become achievable, unless people did what we were doing, getting into a car or hitch-hiking and discovering wherever their feet led them. Back in England, people dreamed of getting as far as the coast. Even that was a major event, and there were many of us at school who had never seen the sea, and bear in mind that in England nowhere is further than 150 kms or so from the coast. So for us to be standing in sight of the ancient Pyramids was unbelievable except that there we stood and what we were looking at were Pyramids thousands of years old and we were just young pups. And in a flash, the antiquity of the Clock Tower and St Albans Cathedral was put in perspective. They were very recent additions and, by comparison, the Cathedral was a dolls' house. Here we stood, in the land of ancient myths and legends, of the Pharaohs and the beauty of Cleopatra (though apparently she hadn't been very beautiful at all), with our vision being gently rocked in the cradle of history. Yes, Logan, you'll go far. The struggle to get there made the reward of being there at least ten times more valuable. When signing that form in Gibraltar, we did in fact almost sign our own death warrants, but that was only a small part of this adventure of a lifetime, and who else did we know who had got this far under their own steam? No one. Time to indulge ourselves and savour the glory.

By the time I was fifteen or sixteen years old, Elvis Presley alone had changed the face of music. Out of that influence appeared the very British Cliff Richard - everyone loves a home town boy (even though he was born in Lucknow, India). He became a pop idol in England and after that worldwide. People told me that I looked like him, and in a way I did, but without his soft face, and, though I love singing, also without his voice. I used Brylcreem to get my hair to look like his. When working at Halfords, I was often in the shop window, fixing up the display shelves, to make it look good and encourage customers in. Girls would stop and gaze at me, and put both their hands to their mouths and do that funny little jump up and down thing that young girls do when surprised by someone famous and popular. It used to flatter me, and that was OK. They waved and blew kisses and I waved back and looked really really cool. If they wanted me, they knew where I worked and they only had to ask. As I mimed the words of Cliff's latest hit - maybe *Living Doll* - through the plate glass window I could hear them squeaking, "Oh. It's Cliff. Marjorie, it's Cliff." But they became a public nuisance as far as the manager was concerned. And not only that, they caused a rapid decline in my productivity. He was forced, on not a few occasions, to go out and chase them away, telling them that, no, he isn't Cliff Richard and please, girls, tell your friends that, no, he isn't Cliff Richard. This young man has a job to do. We need customers, not a fan club on the doorstep!

A long way from the Pyramids and Cleopatra, you might think. But not really, no, because just as we parked the car in the car park close to the Pyramids in Egypt, a coach load of tourists arrived. Derek and I were strolling towards History with a capital H when four or five girls got out of the coach and came running towards us. They were somewhat over-excited, squealing, "Oh, I don't believe it. Look, look! It's Cliff. It's Cliff. Oh, I think I am going to faint." Derek knew he wasn't the focus of this exceptional attention because he and too much of his head of hair had already parted company so that he could no longer even part his hair. I seemed to be growing taller - having an international fan club does that - from my average height to two metres plus the rest in seconds. But there comes the moment of truth. "Sorry darlings. Mistaken identity. My name's Denis Logan, but you can call me Den." I smile a celebrity smile onto their crestfallen faces. They wouldn't believe me, until I pointed out the twelve year old Ford Prefect without a chauffeur and one door handle missing. It's hard disappointing fans. I wonder what the soldiers in Algeria would have made of that scene! As their faces drop and they look at me accusingly, Derek gazes heavenwards, like, "Oh Lord, whatever next!" He wasn't the jealous type but I am sure he thought, "I wish!" As for me, I could only regret that those beauties in Monte Carlo hadn't made the same mistake.

The fear was that the charge to explore a Pyramid in Egypt would be a heavy hit to our finances. ('Finances' is a fancy word, since we had little left but small change and a few bills of doubtful value.) But who could go to New York and not visit the Empire State Building, or Paris and snub the Eiffel Tower, or St Albans and fail to at least catch a glimpse of Blacksmiths Lane? But, surprisingly, even to us, the charge was minimal, well within our budget. We might even do it twice. We bought the ticket which came with a guide. He didn't look very convincing - the Pyramid was looking horribly steep. He was around seventy years old and in those long white Arab robes. He set off, up the edge of the great stones. We had assumed he would go at a fairly leisurely pace, and wheeze and creak, but he hurdled up like a mountain goat and we couldn't keep up with him. About half way up (and it is steep, let me tell you) I had to shout after him to slow down and wait for us (maybe Cliff Richard would have done the same thing). A few more metres and we would be on top of a Pyramid! What I would see was not something I had anticipated, but what else was there that I hadn't anticipated. Photographs of the Pyramids give the impression that the four edges come to a point at the top. That is an illusion. As you know, if you look along the railway tracks, the lines appear to meet at the horizon. Pyramids, or this one anyway, had a flat top, about two or three metres square. Having a camera would have got both of us shot in Algeria, but standing on top of that

Pyramid I longed for a camera. Just to stand there under the sun and look out across Egypt, a view the pharaohs would have had, not to mention all those who sadly died during the construction of this monolithic memorial, that had to be worth at least one photo. But it was not to be.

Unknowingly, we had cheated death by not having the one instrument that would have recorded one of, if not the one greatest moment of my life so far. So I had to record those feelings in my heart and my memory and now, at last, I can write the memory down - I am sure you can imagine how you would feel, at twenty-one years old, after driving all the way across Africa, to find yourself standing in the sun on top of one of the wonders of the world. But there was better still to come. The ticket included visiting the Tomb of Tutankhamen.

A couple of thousand years ago, the Romans had already understood about central heating. (We still delude ourselves that we are modern.) Even earlier than that, the Egyptian architects (and possibly many other architects) understood air-conditioning - it has just taken us a few thousand years to catch up, like me catching up with the tour guide. We explored the chambers hidden beneath all that stone. It was much cooler inside with precisely cut shafts designed to create airflow. Everywhere we looked could be seen places where the alabaster had been scraped from the interior walls across the centuries. The tunnels are very low and you have to move along slowly, always crouched until you emerge in one of the larger chambers. After crouching for a long while in long narrow tunnels, the sense of intense relief coming into a large free space is inspiring, and a surprise. A Pyramid is no place to have a bout of claustrophobia. It is also a shock coming back into the sunshine and the heat. You walk away reluctant to distance yourself from such a glorious feeling of awe and admiration for the race of people who produced such grand constructions that performed so many functions, thousands of years before the races of northern Europe had figured out how to keep pleasantly warm in a very cold climate. It was impossible not to be wonder-struck.

We returned to Cairo and, possibly on a high after the Pyramid experience, we went for broke and entered the Egyptian Museum on Tahrir Square, which we came across by chance - as usual, we had no idea where we were. Into Aladdin's cave once more. I found it close to overwhelming, standing so close to such beautiful works, some of them homely and many of them mind-blowing, so much gold; funeral masks, jewellery, sculpture, and amazingly preserved clothing of those days and ages long gone. I did not know then and I still do not know very much about the history of the people of that part of the world, but I walked away with my view of the world changed forever. I had seen dust and I had seen gold: I had as good as died in the sand, and another human being helped me, and Derek, back to life with a hot bath and a clean bed. I had been intimidated by soldiers, and feared the worst, and I had been welcomed around a campfire by soldiers, and felt protected. Divisions still remain for me totally pointless and, probably, totally unnecessary. And I had learned from where this sense of division arises: it's simply from forgetting that water, food and shelter are finest when shared. I told myself that I may not have had a full education at school, but that this journey had already given me experiences infinitely more precious than anything a 'full education' could give me. And this educational journey, I realised, was my life as just me. In so many ways I was the same as everyone else, and everyone else was the same as me. And all of history was my history, and my history was all there was. I belonged but I couldn't stay.

## Dr. Anwar, I presume

Being by now creatures of habit, the time came to move, so it was back into and back out of Cairo, find Alexandria and a campsite before darkness fell. I got lost, street after tiresome street. Narrow streets, always bustling, calls to prayer from the minarets, music blaring from radios and live instruments, and left here, dither, right there, and Derek was beginning to lose his rag, the first time that had happened since we had been on the road. Finally I told him to cool down, that I'd go and make enquiries from a group of people I'd seen outside a house. I had spotted someone who looked like he might be European, and might even speak English. I had spotted him because he wore a white suit. That may have been triggered by a recollection of Ken the BP man. Perhaps men dressed in white suits were people I should pay attention to.

I walked across the street. I had decided to speak normal English as if I was in St Albans, and hope.

"Good evening folks. My name's Den. My friend's over there in the beige car. I'm sorry to trouble you but we're lost and looking for the way out of Alexandria, and a campsite. Which way should we go?"

The man in the white suit looked completely thrilled, beaming a smile at me.

"Are you English?" It was as if he had at last found an Englishman right on the point of giving up after an exhausting search.

"Yes," I said, shaking his hand, hugely relieved at this stroke of luck, and hearing my own language.

"Very pleased to meet you, Mr. Den. I am Dr. Anwar. I studied medicine in London. Please, you must stay and have coffee with us and tell me the news of London."

Did we know each other already? Yet again I discovered that the most reliable passport, with which I could go anywhere, was not the dark blue one with the Coat of Arms on the cover and the stamps on the pages. My real passport was the smile and my open hand: they didn't have dates on them limiting my right to stay.

"Well, OK, Dr. Anwar, but just coffee. We don't want to be a nuisance."

"No, not at all, Mr. Den, it's a pleasure," he said, putting a friendly hand on my shoulder. "You must stay, so please come inside and accept our hospitality. I was given so much hospitality in London. Now you must accept some of ours. Please. You have travelled such a long way. No need for you to find a campsite. You will stay with us."

Derek was looking through the window, frowning, probably frustrated that this was taking so long. I waved at him, to lock the car and come on over. I introduced him to the doctor and checked with Derek that it was alright with him if we stayed here for a while. We gratefully accepted his offer. Why would we refuse - he was wearing a white suit. He apparently had an apartment across the road and told us to go and bring the car and park it outside. The doctor and his friends or family stood and waited for us. With our overnight gear in our hands we then said goodnight to the others in the group. There was Todero and Anna his wife; Salah, who had a tidy shop about a metre and a half wide, selling fags (yes, I hoped!) and Coke; and finally 'Wakeem the pressman' who did the ironing for the locals.

We followed the doctor up the flight of stairs and he opened the front door. I was very aware that this was only the third front door we had stood in front of since leaving home, the others having been our convalescent home at Grand Hotel, Benghazi, and the bungalow surrounded by a tall iron fence in Tunis. Not having to pitch a tent and boil a can of water on the Gaz burner was a very pleasant plus.

For the people here, and all across North Africa, 'the war' had only come to an end seventeen years before, not very long at all. Amongst all the nations who had fought in Egypt and lost thousands of their sons in the process, the British were very highly regarded, for all their faults and weird ways. Having been born British, and despite never having had to fight off anything much more serious than a cold, we were the fortunate beneficiaries of the high regard that remained at that time.

Passing through the front door we emerged into a large lounge area with a kitchen to the right. We gaped.

"Come through," Dr. Anwar waved us on, "and I'll show you to your room."

We follow him into a large bedroom with two comfortable-looking mattresses on the floor, side by side. We plonked our gear down the way tired travellers do. I had explained to him that I wasn't "Mr. Den", but just plain Den.

"I understand, Den, but don't call me 'doctor'. My name's Anwar. Now, go down the hallway and you'll find the shower room, first door on the right."

I duly went down the hallway, took the first door on the right, opened the door, switched on the light, and felt somewhat bewildered. It was empty, a completely empty space about four metres square. I had to admit that the tiled flooring was impressive, but it was completely empty. Why had he sent me here? I went back to the bedroom.

"Did you find it, Den? First room on the right?"

"Yes, I found it, Anwar, but it's empty. There's nothing in it."

He laughed and told us to come along, he'd show us what I'd missed. How could I have missed anything? The room was empty, all four square metres of beautifully tiled emptiness.

He opens the door, leans in, switches on the light and then presses another switch. Instantly, water sprays down from the far left-hand corner in a huge arc, draining down into a grid in the floor. We gaze in amazement - and I thought the shower at the campsite in France was impressive!

"It's what we call a wet room. It's hot in Egypt too you know."

"Oh, fantastic. I have never seen one of these."

"We're not so backward as you might think." He laughed and winked.

We had a long, long shower, playing around like two kids in such a big space, and then tried to smarten up in 'clean' clothes. Not long after that, Todero came back and took us over to his place for a meal which Anna had prepared, by which time we were almost asleep on our feet. We went back to the apartment, watered and fully fed, and slept until late the next morning. The wonderful blessing of a safe and clean and friendly space in which to rest! The hotel in Benghazi had been an incredible gift, perhaps literally a life-saver, but this was different for being completely personal. Whatever we experience, fortunate or not, there is always something amazing to share, and usually something very, very simple: friendship, a smile, and an open hand. We stayed for a week in our new home in Egypt, accepted into the family as new members and no questions asked. We played football with the locals, Egypt v England - perhaps it was a draw but no one would have cared if it hadn't been, and full-time was when we had had enough. Todero and Anna had three children, the eldest of whom was the very attractive Sandrella, with her brilliant blue eyes and long jet black hair. Her two brothers were Rico (11) and Deco (maybe 7). One evening we went to the local cinema with them all, to watch an American war film. It was in English. While we could relax and follow the action freely and just enjoy the film, the rest of our Egyptian family were having to keep up with the subtitles. They didn't bother us for translations and that left us to enjoy our luxury undisturbed.

Some days Derek and I just wandered the streets of Alexandria on our own. Once, when walking along the harbour shores, we came face to face with two fifteen foot sharks on the beach. That brought us to a stop quick sharp, until we realised that, of course, the sharks were dead. I had never felt a shark's skin, and, being curious as I am, I bent down to stroke it. The skin looks smooth enough, not like a dolphins but my anticipation was rough handled by what felt like 40 grit emery paper. Later on, around 9PM it started to rain heavily, accompanied by deeply rolling thunder and gigantic flashes of lightning which lit up the entire harbour as if it was midday. I had never seen that kind of lightning before either or that intensity of rain.

Early in our stay we noticed another, for us, unusual daily phenomenon. At around noon everything stopped. The maternal Anna would come over and remind us that we needed to go to bed and stay there until 2PM. We were well-behaved boys and followed the advice, lying on our beds sniggering like 5 year-olds. We were looked after by that family as if we were family, and of course by Dr. Anwar as well - I never did feel quite right calling him the bare 'Anwar', and have always referred to him as "Dr" Anwar when telling the stories of my 1001 nights. Lovely food, fresh coffee, if we needed to know something we only had to ask …. to have such company, you know, we couldn't ask for more.

It was evening meal time, everyone seated around the table, Sandrella next to me. She looked at my hand and noticed the ring I was wearing. It had been a 21st birthday present, perhaps worth five English shillings, or €0.30. I slid it off and passed it to her. She took it and looked into her lap. Everyone looked mildly surprised, which surprised me, and then started laughing. What had I done? Having spent years in London as a medical student, Dr. Anwar became interpreter.

"My word, Den." He was laughing hard. "Congratulations. You have just become engaged to be married to the beautiful Sandrella. That's our custom here in Egypt. How long did you mean to stay? Those English girls are going to be so disappointed!"

Sandrella looked at me and laughed as well, but perhaps I saw a little bit of the "I wish" in her eyes. (If she had heard of Cliff Richard, she wasn't letting on.) She gave me the ring back and I rapidly popped it back where it belonged. I felt a little safer then.

It is impossible to imagine how our days in Alexandria could have been better than they were, or with more human people than those who made our stay such a delight and so leisurely. And, dare I say it, after the ordeals we had been through, Derek and I both felt we had kind of earned this lucky break, but we never said that to each other. We felt totally relaxed, at last, and amongst friends even though the only times we spoke English were with Dr. Anwar, but he was busy so those occasions were in fact rather few. On the other hand we felt welcomed and secure with that group of people who had become friends almost instantly. Of course we visited Wakeem and Salah. Maybe language interferes more than we realise.

Wakeem's world, his claimed territory, was a small ground floor room. In that territory, he cleaned and pressed clothes, all by hand, everything and anything that was made of cloth. There were rails with items ready for collection, and piles of stuff to be processed. The only machine was him and his only tool was the iron. It was a confined space and we would drop by, and sit and watch him working. Occasionally he would look across at us – a few arm's lengths away - and smile and talk as if we understood. And occasionally one of his customers would come in, bringing more work for him or to collect and pay for what he had done for them. We were always introduced as he, presumably, told each customer what he knew about us and where we had been. (He would have been kept up to date by what we had shared with Dr. Anwar.) The customer would shake hands with us, smiling, always, and then perhaps wish us a pleasant stay. We never felt 'in the way' and he seemed to be happier when we were around; why that should be I do not know because all we could do was look and smile. I was fascinated by watching his slender hands move, adjusting the fabric or smoothing it to make sure he had done a good job. He was never in a hurry and took great care hanging items up or folding them. Eventually we would excuse ourselves and wander back to the apartment or take a walk along the narrow streets. Wakeem was on the thin side, like me, perhaps because he was always working in the heat and steam.

Salah's world was even smaller than Wakeem's. It was perhaps two metres from back to front and with both arms stretched out you would touch both walls. Basically a hole in the wall with a shutter to bring down at the end of a day's business (always late in the evening), but from that space he earned his keep. And we were as welcome there as we were at Wakeem's, though we went there less often because it was a shop and in shops you spend money and we were trying not to spend money. He had a Coca-Cola cold box on legs and a tiny counter with some sweets on display and a few shelves behind the counter, stocked with cigarettes. One day he did in fact give me a packet - maybe he saw me staring at the temptations - and that packet I have kept to this day. We would stay a short while, and always shake hands when we left, and always that warm smile saw us on our way. When not serving customers, he sat on a stool, smoking, or looking along the street or talking with a friend.

All of them were simply delightful people, Dr. Anwar just a little plump, Todero's wife middle-age rounded, Wakeem thin, Salah even thinner. And however it happened I do not really know, or why, but a bond between us all seemed to grow by the day, a bond that has lasted all the years between then and now. I am sure that if we met again - if they are alive - that bond would come to life again and fill the smiles on our faces and warm the hands that would seal a greeting or a farewell. In that way, this group of ordinary Egyptian people adopted us and that kind of experience only happened that once. I often wonder why.

But all good things - and all the other things too - have to come to an end, and we had to get going again. We went with Dr. Anwar to the shipping company he recommended and booked a passage to Beirut via Cyprus, leaving the following evening at 8PM. The ship was the S.S. Ionia. The tickets, the cheapest we could get, included the car and the two of us: deck class, which literally meant what it said - we would be on the deck and no access to any facilities at all. We paid for the boat to get us to Beirut and that is what it would do, and nothing more than that. No frills? No problems. We were well used to that by now. We arrived at the dock in good time. The family were around us and we pointed out to them that there was our car being hoisted up above the ship in a huge, rope net, some ten metres up in the air and then disappearing down into the hold. And there we were, surrounded by Dr. Anwar, Todero and Anna and their three children, along with Salah the cigarette and Coke man, and Wakeem the pressman. Anna came forward, crying, and gave us a large bunch of flowers. Todero came forward and gave us both a hug and shook our hands, and the children looked the way children do when they say goodbye and do not really know what they're feeling or how to express it. Our eyes were not dry but we did not sob. It was so very hard to turn away from people you feel a deep and clean affection for, especially people who have befriended you simply because you asked for directions to a campsite and you happened to speak English. Salah, though, was quite distressed, tears streaming down his face, and after embracing him and Wakeem everything was a blur until we found ourselves at the railings looking down on a small knot of people trying to make each other feel better.

You say goodbye at the airport terminal, people disappear into the belly of the plane the way our car disappeared into the stomach of the ship, and it's all over. The plane takes off and you can't see anyone inside. But the ship pulls away from the dock slowly. The siren sounds - numbers and letters don't flick over on a huge departure board. The ship eases away from the harbour, and you can still see and wave to those you leave standing there, and they can identify you because you are clearly visible, at the railings waving your handkerchief. The process is slow, like removing a number of stitches, but the wound of the moment of departure is not healed yet, and the process of pulling away is painful for the heart. Finally, the ship is out to sea, and Anna is in the apartment clearing up after our stay. We could write to each other, Dr. Anwar had said. But in a way, there was nothing to say that we hadn't already made perfectly clear, without any room for doubt. The mutual affection had been clear as day. We knew we would all miss each other.

# CHAPTER 7:

# Six feet three and full of muscle

The ship was quite full. We watched as most of the passengers went down to their cabins, until there was just Derek and I and a few others living on the smell of an oil-rag. It was still very hot but we managed to find a large vent of wooden slats where it was marginally cooler and perhaps not a bad place to sleep. We had remembered to bring some food (five bread rolls) and an empty Coke bottle. We would slip down to the toilets and fill that up when we got thirsty. Those supplies were in a carrier bag, which was good. What was not so good was that we had left the carrier bag in the car when it was loaded, and the car was now some long way out of reach in the hold, somewhere in a big big ship. I set off to find the car, not really holding out much hope.

On the way down the between-deck stairway I passed someone who looked like a steward. Using gesture, I demonstrated that I was looking for my car (twist imaginary steering wheel) because that car was somewhere down there (pointing down the stairway) and in the car (opening imaginary door) there was a bag (putting hand into imaginary bag) and in the bag was food (pulling out and eating imaginary food) which was good because I was hungry (rubbing stomach, pulling hungry face). The steward looked at me as if I was not altogether 100%, pointed down the stairway, shrugged and carried on up the stairs. And as he went up, so I went down, and down, and down. (There is something ghostly about the echo of a ship's stairways.) At each level I went through a door and had a look around but no sign of the beige beauty, so down, and down, and down, and there I spotted it, dwarfed by machinery and other freight. (There is something ghostly about the pit of the stomach of the hold of a ship.) I worked my way to it, opened the boot, pulled the piece of string that had been operative since just after getting to Algeria, and opened the door. With the carrier bag in my hand, I locked the door in the essential manner, and I turned to go back, imagining the happy look on Derek's face when I reappear with our vitamin supply (five bread rolls) and the empty Coke bottle. I turned around.

I never really fully turned round as I was surrounded by a group of foreign deck-hands and they were coming towards me, accusingly shouting "Buckshee, buckshee!" or something like that, as I tried to hold on tight to the carrier bag with one hand, showing with the other that my pockets were empty. After about five minutes of this stand-off they reluctantly had to agree: I had little more than the clothes I stood up in. They moved away and I scuttled up the stairway as fast as you can on a ship. It was a long way up and I was in a hurry but I did not forget to fill the Coke bottle up with water when I passed the toilets. I broke out into the open air the way a diver breaks the surface of the sea after a deep hold-your-breath dive. I found Derek - much easier than finding the car.

"At last! What kept you?"

I tell him.

"You and dramas, Den." He shakes his head in disbelief and gets out the rolls.

"Fair enough, but then there's me and men in white suits too."

"Hungry?"

"Not so much hungry now as thirsty. It's a long way down there."

"After you with the Coke then, but wipe the top when you've finished, won't you."

"It's water."

"Let's imagine it's Coke."

It was getting on for one in the morning. We'd been at sea for almost five hours, and only two days and a bit to go. We were both asleep on the wooden vent we had found, curled up like characters from a Dickens' novel. We both woke up with a start.

"You want cabin? You want cabin?"

Standing over us was a big shape, tall, maybe six feet three (two metres plus) and made of muscle, dark skinned, sallow, maybe Greek, wearing a naval cap with a peak.

"You want cabin or no?"

We stared at him, stunned.

"I have cabin for one. You want?"

Derek kind of half lifted up his hands and offered, "We don't have the money for a cabin and that is why we are sleeping on an air vent."

"For this cabin, no money."

We looked at him. He was, as you say, solidly built. I was skinny and perhaps, on times, a tad too bold for my own good. Derek, on the other hand, was shall we say a little introverted, and perhaps, on times, a tad too cautious for his own good. We made a good combo. But we were not scrappers.

We looked at each other. Perhaps we both had the same thought: just maybe, people hire a cabin so that this kind of thing doesn't happen. A wooden vent in the deck does not have a lockable door. Ahh. Right. Yes. Hmm. However, a cabin was a good thought: wooden vents are hard. Cool, but hard. Well, I'll be! Another stroke of luck. In the desert when almost out of water, we had tossed a coin to see who would face possible death first. Being the lucky one of our combo, I won. Surely my luck couldn't hold out. At least we had a coin between us. Derek flipped it up. It spun. As it came down, I called "Heads". And, yes, heads it was. I had won, again.

"Sorry, Degs. See you in the morning. Keep covered up, won't you."

He almost snarled. I smiled and followed my leader in the naval cap with a peak, Mr. six feet plus and full of muscle. Luck just seemed to follow me around. I kept following him for quite a while, along these corridors as nameless as the streets of Alexandria, and down steps - didn't I come down here a short while ago? - and I had no idea how I would get back to that vent in the morning.

We reached a door. Mr. Muscle opened the door, rudely. He proposed by gesture that I should enter. I did enter, since, after all, the idea of sleeping on a mattress was a good idea, wasn't it, and Derek was jealous. I did what you always do after entering your hotel bedroom door: you close it. Mr. Muscle, however, had come in. I still didn't twig that something might not be quite as I would like. I was a man who liked girls, I liked girls who thought I was Cliff Richard and I liked girls in Monte Carlo even though they didn't think I was Cliff Richard. I had liked Sandrella, but she was too young. Girls were good. You could perhaps marry a girl one day, and be happy, and even make babies. What was he doing? Why was he hanging around. Couldn't he see that I was man enough to take care of myself? I knew I was man. People regularly reminded me, years ago, that I was man now: You're a man now, Logan, and it's time for you to go out in the world and get a job. Go do it! And I answered the phones and walked around with sealed envelopes.

I checked the cabin out. It was no more than three metres square, and had a single bed, and a very large porthole, above the waterline. Hardly room enough to swing a dead cat by the tail. I was having to think faster than my brain was inclined to go. My brain was not keeping up with play. Then a thought rang out: Going deck class does indeed mean that you get on the ship, but it also means that you do not get on the passenger list. Deck class is like cargo and the cargo in our case was the car and not us. But then that thought sort of ran away, probably frightened by what was obvious but which I couldn't see. My thinking had more sense than I did! No doubt about it, this fellow here was a man, every inch a man, huge, the epitome of manliness, a lady killer. Lucky guy him, I thought, as I took off my t-shirt and shorts. I imagined he was simply being polite, making sure I was nicely settled, and then he'd say whatever Greeks say for 'night-night dear', turn off the light and go, closing the door quietly behind him.

For some reason, and not a conscious reason, I left my underpants on, and jumped into bed, as you do. By the bed was a bedside table, just like in the movies, and on the bedside table was a magazine, as you would expect if paying for a cabin on a cruise ship to Beirut. I picked up the magazine and pretended to read. The bed seemed quite comfortable, not that you could bounce on it or anything like that, but it did have a certain comfort compared with the wooden ventilator slats which were probably playing havoc with Derek's vertebrae. Poor old Derek. Not to worry, chum, one day you'll get as lucky as me! I peaked out from behind the magazine, only to see Mr. Muscle stripping down. He was all muscle. Oh dear God. My blood went cold. Thoughts froze inside my head. Deck class, not on passenger list; port hole (large) above waterline; corpse out of port hole (plop), no one any the wiser, and goodbye Mr. Logan and sorry about that, chum.

Mr. Muscle climbed into the bed, the single bed. What to do? I didn't want to see his face so I turned over and pressed myself against the wall, as you do when there are two in a single bed and space is at a premium and the space you want to stake out as no man's land should prevent touching. I was saying to myself, "Well, you may be a lady killer, mate, but let me make this very clear to you, sir, you are not going to get a hold of my willie, so let's get that straight. Do you get my drift or do I have to spell it out?" We had coped with signing our lives away in Gibraltar. We had coped with sometimes painful hunger - biscuits do not make you feel full of beans. We had coped with guns in our faces. We had survived nearly dying of thirst. We had been befriended by nomads who might just as easily have cut our heads off and had a good laugh. We had slept on a minefield, slept like lambs. We had survived near-death from sunstroke. Why had I been so lucky and called 'Heads' and won a night with Mr. Muscle? Why? Why? Why?

The light went out. One of those strings with a knot in the end. It was pitch black. My eyes were screwed shut. I was screaming my way through the imaginary rosary of my good fortune. Hail mary mother of god hail mary mother of god hail mary mother of god. Help me please, please help me hail mary mother of god. His leg, presumably his left leg, bared, dragged its way over my buttocks. Thank God for my underpants. Hail mary mother of god, hail mary mother of god, what do I do!? Run, my son, run. Run for your very life, or your arse will be in a sling. I groped for the light string, faking seasickness, clutching my mouth as if I was going to be sick all over him. I leaped off the end of the bed, ready to be violently, but violently ill, and I grabbed my sandals and I clutched at my clothes and I opened the door and I slammed it behind me, violently, and I ran, I ran, I ran, I ran.

Scrape a car along a wall and the bodywork has scratches to prove it. My faith in human nature, perhaps in my own nature, had taken a hit. For a long while after that, I felt a little more wary. No disrespects to anyone, even Mr. Muscle. But I had been profoundly shocked, perhaps, at the end of the day, by my own naivety. In the meantime, I found Derek who was half asleep, safely, stiffly, maybe happily. I curled up against the wall next to the ventilator, and shook. I trembled, as if I was very cold. Now and again I stood by the railings and listened to the water against the side of the ship. For the first time for a long time, I felt vulnerable, pathetically vulnerable. I felt haunted, stirred, shaken, and spat out. I didn't sleep that night. I couldn't even doze off. Perhaps my luck had run out. But there again, I had not come to actual harm. Had I? Had I been a woman I would have been raped. All I knew was that I was not quite so vulnerable as a woman, but it is a very fine line.

The ship docked at Lemesos, Cyprus, and stayed there for a couple of hours. Derek asked me what had happened the previous night and I told him that I didn't want to talk about that but one day I would and that he had won the better night's sleep. He didn't make an issue of it. I couldn't laugh it off. We had a bread roll each and a few sips of water from the Coke bottle, and the ship set sail again.

"If we need water, Derek, do you mind going down and getting it next time."

"No, sure."

"Thanks. It's a long way down there."

Beirut. Another bustling port. The rain was falling heavily but it was warm. Looking way down from the deck I noticed the toy figure of a Greek man in black oilskins and a naval cap with a peak, supervising the docking and unloading process. I shivered. Once down the gangplank we waited for the off-loading of our car, patiently waiting for it to appear in its rope nest on its way from the hold where I had heard the word 'buckshee' when clutching a humble carrier bag with bread rolls and an empty Coke bottle in it, waiting for it to dangle overhead as it had done in Alexandria, and then get lowered slowly and gently to earth again, quayside, where Dr. Anwar would not be waiting to say hello. "Be gentle with our baby, won't you. That car's been good to us. It's our home."

# CHAPTER 8:

# No paperwork, bogged down anyway

*(In May 1960 Turkey experienced a military coup d'état against the democratically elected government of the Democrat Party. It was short-lived; the military junta returned power to civilians in October 1961.)*

When we examined the car quayside at Beirut, we found that the rope net had managed to pull the exhaust pipe from the manifold. We reported that at the Harbour Office (more paperwork) and ended up with around the equivalent of €2. We managed to repair the damage ourselves with a length of thick wire, but even so the exhaust functioned well enough until we arrived at our final port of call, still a long way off. The compensation money was converted into petrol in the tank, and we just drove, through Lebanon, and slept, and drove, through Syria where we thought we were back in the Sahara except that the roads were slightly better, and over the comparatively short distance to the Turkish border.

We were heading north again after a whole continent of going predominantly east. Even though the blow was softened by the week with Dr. Anwar and his friends, the blow of realising we couldn't go through Israel had nudged New Zealand off the map for us. Added to which we were seriously low on funds and the car was starting to show signs of wear and tear. If the car broke down, we would be in a very grave situation. Walking to New Zealand was impossible, for me and Derek anyway. Walking to Northern Europe was not quite so far. So we cut our cloth. Added to which we ourselves were beginning to feel the wear and tear as well: we had been on the road for longer than either Derek or I could remember. We had become nomads, like most of humanity. Each day we moved a little further, further into our own selves, and maybe the scenery changed, and maybe it didn't. Did we really want to go to New Zealand? Not really, no. The idea had taken us out of our comfort zone and brought us through experiences that were already changing us, had already changed us and how we looked at life. The petrol tank might be full, but we were starting to feel more out of gas than we had been when we started. We did not have a bad feeling about heading north; in a way, recognising limits is part of the process, and we were recognising what those limits were, for us, in our circumstances as they were then. We wouldn't regret it, just as we would never regret a single mile that we had covered, and that we had yet to cover, just as, so far, we had no reason to regret a single action we had done. There is a wonderful power in that feeling. We had made friends with, and been befriended, by life itself. We were still in our early-mid twenties but already knew how meaningless age is.

We passed fairly quickly from Lebanon into Syria, staying close to the coast as that was the shortest route to Turkey. And the only moment of real note was when we drove alongside a field. Perhaps it was a result of the accumulated strain of our journey across Africa, but we had noticed a change of mood in each other. That could also have been because, after our experience of Africa, we felt safer than we had for a while. Basically we were content to drive and look through the windows of the car, and take a break when we felt like it. And this spot seemed like a good place for a break, even just for the pleasure of looking across a field of plants growing after what felt like years of staring at sand change shape. The plants here looked like they were growing white tennis balls, but more fluffy than tennis balls. We had a little wander to stretch our legs. On closer inspection, the tennis balls turned out to be cotton.

"Hey, Degs. Let's stay awhile. I'll spin you up a few t-shirts. What's your favourite colour?"

(Never having been in a cotton field before - or since - I picked a couple of tennis balls, and still have them although they are no longer white and fluffy; they are light grey and flat.)

We had become quite adept at border crossings and the Turkish border was just another one, another stamp, some more paperwork, another language, another quality of scenery, another glimpse of how people fashion their lives and how the landscape fashions them. Turkey is a mountainous country, with reasonable roads (and no sand hiding them), and we headed for a town called

Konya. We were on the coast, some distance before a village called Antalya, single tracks with steep drops, even sheer drops down to the sea in places. Perched between a mountainside and the sea down there, we come round a bend and I slammed on the brakes. There was a huge pile of boulders and rubble in front of us, under which pile was where the road had been: a landslide had torn it off and thrown it down into the sea, like paperwork into the waste bin. We got out nervously to check around the car. The pile of rubble was literally at the edge of what was basically a cliff. Had we not been able to stop in time or been going any faster, the car would simply have bounced off the pile and tumbled down into the sea, as the road had already done. Had it been night-time, well, that would most likely have been lights out with a vengeance. The track was too narrow so we couldn't turn around. Reversing all the way we had come was impossible so we decided to reverse until the landscape flattened out and we could perhaps drive across country and chance on an alternative route. That's what happened and we were driving across fields, carefully, but what's a field or two after thousands of kilometres of desert. In the distance we saw a village. Never say die: where there's a village, there's probably a road, and there will certainly be people. We pressed on more slowly not so much out of caution as because the ground became softer, in fact until the ground became very muddy, in fact until the rear wheels starting spinning and then gave up spinning because the rear axle was kissing the earth for all it was worth and had become embedded. Full stop.

For every downside there's an upside? Sometimes you are forced to wonder whether that is true. Well, the car may be stuck, but we still had legs and a village was in sight, so all was not lost, yet. Plus, if the worst came to the worst, there were two of us anyway and we could tell each other jokes until …. well, until nothing was funny any more, and we had had some practice at that. We didn't step out of the car; we kind of slid out because we were pretty much at ground level. So here we are, Derek: Turkey awaits us or lies in wait. Thick mud has enormously different properties to drifted sand but both of the surfaces are heavy going. Grey sky over a mountainous terrain makes you feel a different person than the one in which you were brought to your knees by a blistering, merciless midday sun. Time for the coin?

"It's fine, Degs. I'll go."

Having become accustomed to staggering across sand and rocks, I now re-learned the way you negotiate mud, slipping, sliding, kicking excess off the bottoms of the shoes, feeling the muscles strain with each step and trying not to fall over. And I wasn't even carrying two heavy water bags. The village reminded me of Dickens' *Oliver*. Oldie worldie cuddlie charm and quaint old stone and beam houses that seemed crude, small and frail after the pyramids, but still not as frail as a shack of flattened 50 gallon oil drums, and yet not as amenable or flexible as a nomad's tent. No better door when desperate than the first one you come to. I knocked. Perhaps the door was very heavy or the hinges were tired and rusted because that door opened very slowly, so slowly that perhaps it would just shut again, but it didn't. An old man came out. I must have looked quite a sight, legs all muddy and my hair lacking a little Brylcreem and a comb's caress. He didn't speak, and nor did I. Instead, he watched as I gestured, pointing across the fields to over there, can you see it, that car, that's my car, our car, and it's very very stuck, in your very muddy field. I made a tug-of-war gesture and heaved and he got the point. Now it was his turn and, without a word, he gestured for me to follow him. So far so good. I trailed after him as he went from house to quaint little house telling everyone there was work to be done. Soon there's a posse of some fifteen men and some of their children who had a long length of thick rope leading two mules pressed into service. At the bare edge of life, language can be a luxurious encumbrance, like too much mud on your boots. Here there was a problem that had been quickly understood and people are alive to solve problems and off we trudged to solve one. They seemed more at home in mud than I did; for the children it was as natural as sand and rock was for some other children I had met. It was what life had given them.

Derek's eye were popping out of his head, as he leaned with one hand against the useless, distance guzzling beige Ford Prefect. What a sight it must have been for him, to see this composite tow truck of two-legged and four-legged beasts of burden coming towards him. And perhaps just as ropes might have helped haul massive stones of a pyramid into place, the rope was tied around the front bumper of our chariot, the other end to the mules' harness and the children led the mules and the rugby team of men pushed from behind, and, just like that, the car popped out of the mud, like a bee from the hive. Hats in the air, loud cheering, children jumping up and down, hugs, handshakes, thumps on the back - these people were hardy - and Derek carefully drives the rest of the way across to the village and the road, while the crowd followed along behind and alongside the trophy. Landslide, a lucky escape, bogged down and a touch of desperation, knock on a door, people emerge out of nowhere, wheels back on road surface, and job done. Of course we couldn't possibly leave without sharing a coffee with them and letting the children poke around the car and look at us with their daring and their shy faces. They weren't surprised to see us: they were delighted to see us. We had no language to share, but it was as if they were saying, "Den! Derek! At last. We have been waiting for you two for longer than we can remember. But, you know, you didn't have to drive across the fields to our back door; you should have come to the front door. Ah, you English! You do make life very difficult for yourselves sometimes."

We felt good, and reluctant to leave, but the traveller must travel - it comes with the territory. So we ploughed on, so to speak, after they had explained where we had to go, and then we reached Konya the way we obviously would. Old place and very nice. Not big. Medium. I like medium. We would stay there the night. Camping. We were good at camping. But first of all we bought some eggs and bread and wandered around in no hurry at all. Shops, people, no boiling hot sun, no dust, and the occasional facility like a toilet. Africa? Where's that? It was pleasantly warm, and after pitching the tent and setting up the car security system (string is good, string is humble) we strolled into town, sat at a café and actually purchased a coffee each, a small contribution to the local economy. And we sat and looked out over the beautiful surroundings these people lived amongst. We both quietly took stock. As far as things went, like objects, there wasn't a great deal to take stock of: it had nearly all gone. But in terms of living, well, I am still taking stock of all that.

We noticed a great many people were walking past the coffee shop, going off down the street, and, after a while, they came back and walked past again. They were promenading. When we'd finished our drinks we'd join them. It was the community evening out, everyone dressed clean and casual, conversation as they walked, hello to those they knew passing the other way or standing in shops, or at the windows of their homes, no one in a hurry, tomorrow can do what it likes but for today they were OK thank you, and Konya was an OK place to be. Yes, we could drink to that. The world is as big as the human heart that opens to it or as small as the bullet or the vicious word that brings the heart to a standstill.

# CHAPTER 9:

# The meaning of green

The journey from Egypt via Cyprus to Turkey had not been without incident. It had been sad leaving Egypt; the voyage on the Ionia for me had been challenging if not mildly traumatic; in Turkey we had again imagined we had come too close to the edge of disaster. But the stage after that was relaxing. Heading from Konya to Ankara we took it easy, enjoying the scenery, driving slowly, taking our time getting the camp set up, and not being concerned if we woke up later than we had been in the habit of doing.

Hamlets, villages, towns and cities slipped past the window and that was all the same to us. Ankara came and went. We had by now firmly changed our focus from the antipodes to Northern Europe, but we still kept our eyes open. Istanbul could not be ignored and we stopped there for a while to check it out - we wouldn't be passing this way again in a hurry - and for the second time we adopted the disguise of tourists, as we had done at the pyramids. So we wandered, amongst the cafés and the ever-present smell of strong coffee, with groups of men sitting smoking strange pipe things out of odd-shaped bottles (those contraptions reminded me of bagpipes), past carpet shops where people haggled. Everywhere we heard people haggling for a better deal, squeezing a bargain out. And always we could look up and see white minarets. Water was easy to come by - water and petrol had become engraved at the top of our list of priorities - as was cheap bread, so we stocked up. We came, we saw, and we carried on.

From there we passed through Ipsala and the Greek border and Thesalonika, and left them behind as we followed the amazingly beautiful coast road. We felt good and the Ford Prefect still hummed along. The sea was an exquisite blue-turquoise, and the sky a completely different blue to the sky over the desert we had crossed and which we remembered all too clearly. The two landscapes had one thing in common: goats, goats around every bend. But around one bend there was more than the anticipated collection of goats: a collection of roofs just above the surface of the earth, a village of roofs. It turned out to be a cemetery of ancient coffins or small mausoleums, and was obviously an ancient place. At the next town we stopped to camp, enjoying once again a balmy evening promenading with the local people. After that our traditional five-course meal of coffee and bread, and zip up the tent and off to sleep. We came, we saw, we carried on.

The next day found us heading for Skopje in what was the unified Yugoslavia at the time. The condition of the roads was much better than we had experienced for quite a while and, taking advantage of that, we just drove, through nightfall and into the night. The roads were unlit so it was a pleasant relief to pass through a small town or village, all of them quite picturesque even at night. But around 10 or 11PM we noticed a green light flashing in the distance. Not thinking much of it and not knowing what to think of it, we cruised on through the dark, keeping at a steady speed comfortably below the limit. The green light kept flashing now and again as we got closer and closer. We knew that a red light meant Stop and a green light meant Go, all over the world. Up ahead we saw two cars that had pulled over, and as we flashed past them the green light flashed, and we kept going, as you do when seeing a green light. Green light means Go, doesn't it?

Some four minutes later it became evident that a car was catching us up at some considerable and increasing speed. Sooner than we had thought, the car overtook us, pulled in ahead of us and slowed down, giving us no option but to do the same. We followed it to the side of the road and stopped. Recent memories floated back up. A uniformed policeman climbed out of the car ahead, lit up by our headlights. He had his right hand on the pistol in the holster on his hip. The lack of foreign language skills had stood us in good stead so far, and we had become quite efficient at saving our breath by developing our gesture-skills. Confident we had not broken a speed limit, had been driving on the appropriate side of the road and done nothing more offensive than drive past a green flashing light, I wind down the passenger window, to give friendly greeting with the palms of both hands raised and facing the figure. He barks. After passing through so many countries, I was by now street-wise, and was utterly convinced that this armed man could not be asking whether me and my friend were having a pleasant evening in Yugoslavia. If he didn't wish to meet us, he most definitely wanted us to get out of the car before he had to do something else which we might regret.

We got out. He waved Derek round to the same side of the car, shouting as if we were presumably deaf. He continued shouting, incorporating gesture-talk as well as we could have hoped to. He gestured, shouting to amplify his gestures. He didn't need to work himself up into a frenzy; he was in a frenzy when he had been chasing us. We must turn the car around and go back to where we had most recently come from. We in turn indicated, with less force but just as much clarity, that he was mistaken perhaps, because we had every intention of going the way the car was facing. It was probably not pressing itself in on his thinking, but he was outnumbered, two to one. We continued to gesture-argue in this fashion for what must have been half an hour. All of a sudden he reached breaking point, let out a torrent of what must have been choice Yugoslavian swearing, threw his hands in the air, paced off to his car door, got in, slammed the door and burned rubber doing a U-turn, spitting stones all over the road. And off into the night he went. He had probably come to the end of his shift and didn't need us to ruin his evening any further. We scratched our heads, had a laugh, and set off in the direction which to us seemed preferable. Another 80 kms further on, we called it a day, pitched camp, and drifted off, our lights going out like headlamps when the battery has gone flat.

Not long after dawn the next day, we checked the car over before setting out. Oil was OK, and water needed topping up but other than that the car appeared in good shape still and the exhaust pipe had stayed in place. On we went. Our eyes seemed to enjoy the European trees and the variety of scenery; not familiar territory but refreshing. Why it happened where it did I don't know but on going over a bridge we both noticed the mileage reading: 99,994. In those days the mileometer went up to 99,999 and then returned to zero. We pulled off the road when it showed five zeros. It was perhaps symbolic, that we had reached some kind of new beginning. Not long after that we spotted thick green green grass by the side of the road. We stopped, ran over and lay down on it with our arms and legs stretched out as if we were floating on the sea. I had not realised just how much I had missed something so simple and once so familiar and as beautiful as thick green grass. It felt so very good to my hands, my eyes and my nose. Ah, the smell of humble grass!

Our minds were turning towards the world we had known and that gave us the impetus to cover distance rather than keep stopping. We really had nothing left to sell, except what we needed in order to survive - the back seat no longer had clothes on it, and the trunk was only looking after the camping gear. Our single major asset was the car. Stop and spend: drive on and save. In that frame of mind we by-passed Belgrade and visualised ourselves by-passing Zagreb, crossing over the Alps and into West Germany, to Munich, Stuttgart, Luxembourg, Belgium, Ostende and across the Channel/North Sea. Somewhere around Zagreb there would be cause for concern.

# CHAPTER 10:

# Backwards to Christmas

We had had good reason to be thankful that the design of the Ford Prefect engine was so user-friendly, so easily accessible in the event of needing to look for contraband arms or cameras or needing to fix something. Many of those running repair tasks that now cost a fortune could be done by most people with some basic knowledge of how a motor engine works and where the bits are. So far neither the engine nor the rest of the car had let us down, despite collisions with the occasional sand-dune, piles of tarmac and a landslide. But on going up a slight hill near Zagreb the engine was not humming quite so sweetly. In fact, the engine sounded tired, as if it had realised, after the event, that the mileometer had returned to its factory setting which could only mean that it needed a rest. The loss of power was even noticeable on the flat. And we had the Alps ahead of us. It was late Autumn and heading into winter. Maybe our ears were deceiving us - or we did not want to hear what we were hearing - but going down through a gear when you ought to be going up through a gear (or vice-versa), well, that couldn't be a good sign.

After a couple more hills, we found a spot to pull over and stopped.

We opened the bonnet and propped it up on the metal stick. Looking into the piece of machinery that had brought us so far, we could be forgiven for feeling some affection for this ingenious collection of metal and wires and tubes: our lives had depended on it. We examined the patient, hoping that there would be no symptoms that would indicate that the patient might have to go into pre-op and then the operating theatre itself. Heaven forbid. But, no, no wires were loose, no tubes were loose or perishing, and the distributor leads were all in good shape. That meant that the cause of our losing power, even in the two low gears - there was only one high one, third or top gear - the only cause could be that an exhaust valve had burned out and the engine was down to three of the four cylinders. That diagnosis meant that from now on we would be restricted to about 60 kms an hour, and that on the ascent side of mountains or gentle slopes one of us might have to pedal like hell and the other one get out and push. From Zagreb across the Alps? That's a long way. We had noticed that the air was a lot colder these nights and the Alps were, well, yes, kind of high up there. The challenges that had been offered by the summer heat of the desert and the absence of water would now be replaced by the cold of the approaching winter, the altitude that we would have to reach, and the presence of water in the form of snow. But, we told each other, one step at a time and each bridge as it comes.

Passing through Austria the scenery let us forget the challenges for a while. Such a beautiful country, with the snow-capped mountains, deep valleys, picturesque villages and the charm of the houses with their steep roofs, all nestling comfortably into the landscape. With each mile we were climbing higher and with the engine reduced to about 75% efficiency our rate of forward progress was sinking lower. The engine had started to struggle to convert energy consumed into headway achieved, and the sheer grandeur of the fantastic views had less and less of a compensatory effect on our worsening personal outlook as we negotiated sharper and steeper hairpin bends, uphill and downhill. We had ample cause for concern. About a kilometre up ahead there appeared to be a summit, much as the blue rind of ocean had appeared to be just past the summit of the next dune. We reached the 'summit' only to see a few more summits. The engine was seriously overheated. The road was good and dry, but either side was dressed with a blanket of snow. We stopped at the lookout point and turned the engine off. From the pyramids to this! Staggering views! Man on top of pyramid. Man on top of snow-clad summit. Life with extremes wherever you go, and us somewhere between them and all the other contradictions. Den and Derek and a Ford Prefect, beige. Beige? Yes, beige, beige isn't that much more obvious to the eye in snow country than it is amongst sand dunes. Walking off into snow country and will the same 'fifty metres from camp' rule still apply? We were not about to try that one!

For a good half an hour we absorbed the panorama that, in nature, is only available from the tops of high dunes or pyramids, high mountains or from ships at sea. We checked the engine; it was still warm and the radiator obviously needed topping up, so off came the radiator cap and in went handfuls of snow. (How we would have welcomed snow in Libya!) It was early afternoon but already quite chilly. What we had left for clothing was what we were wearing: jeans, shirt and t-shirt. We were in the Alps. That was a concern but little we could do about it unless we started wearing a sleeping bag each. Our trip so far had been self-funding, converting possessions into fuel for the car or for us. We had nothing left to self-fund with. We took a deep breath and set off again for what had to be 'the summit'. The climb was steep, very steep, very very steep, and slow, and slower still, until the steepness could not be overcome by the fading power of our noble engine. Just as a stone reaches the top of its ascent and momentarily hovers before starting the descent at an ever increasing speed, so we came to the top of our upward progress and came to a stop. Unlike the stone, the car has a handbrake. Derek applied the handbrake. Clearly this moment's pause had been given to us so that we could put our two heads together and come up with an answer. We had had moments like that before, and had come to decisions very amicably, and here we were on the side of a mountain in Austria to prove just how effective those decisions had been. Not necessarily wise but effective.

Derek, at twenty-five years old, was the senior partner of the well-seasoned Jakeman-Logan team. He was taller than Den who was a mere twenty-one years old, and the junior partner. Derek was also much heavier than Den, weighing in, as Derek did, around the 95 kg mark, a heavyweight without the muscle and all that skipping practice. Being more inclined to common sense than Den, Derek pointed out, with perfect logic, that his weight in the car was creating undesirable resistance for the engine to overcome, never mind the steepness of the ascent and the contributing factor of humble gravity. Den concurred, not in a servile manner either: he was simply too tired to argue and, anyway, the logic was crystal clear and could not be gainsaid. That incisive logic insisted that Derek walk up the rest of the mountain (which was mainly hairpin bends) while Den took over the driving. But before Den jumped into action in his keenness to contribute, Derek had one more point of logic to sharpen. As the vehicle had most recently come to rest, while going uphill, without the aid of braking power, or encountering an obstacle such as had been encountered in earlier days, and since the vehicle had been in a forward gear at the time, the deduction had to be made that the forward gears were, to put it bluntly, useless. Derek asked Den whether he could find any flaw in that line of argument. Den's mind was somewhere else but, no, he had to agree that, so far, Derek's reasoning was, sadly, spot on, razor sharp, incontrovertible or however one said things like that about logic as watertight as a shark's skin. And Derek then only had one more deduction to deduce. And Den wondered what indeed that might be. And Derek sighed - for this was not good news. And then he spoke. What it means, my good friend, is that you, my right hand man, Den Logan, will be required to drive the rest of the way up this mountain in reverse gear, on the right side but which is still for us the wrong side of the road, and looking over your shoulder. Den needed little time to accept the brutal logic. But Derek had a word of warning. He explained to Den, who was all ears, that he should take it slowly, be sure not to make any sudden over-corrective twists of the steering wheel and press over zealously on the accelerator because, he explained, should you disappear over the edge there probably isn't much between you and the car and sea-level, and that was a long, long way down. Den was starting to shiver, not from fear, simply from the cold. He was anxious to get out of the wind. They were both agreed that this plan was a good plan. In fact it was the only plan.

Derek fetched the sole surviving blanket from the trunk, and wrapped it about his person. Den remarked that dressed thus in the blanket Derek had a vague resemblance to people high up in the mountains in Peru although it was true that Peruvians are not often seen in their native habitat decked out in tartan blankets. Humour in what could be desperate circumstances takes the edge off the shock that might be just around the corner. On his walk up to the summit, Derek was going to adopt the same principle as racing drivers: he would follow the shortest line between coming out of one bend and going round the next. This might entail covering some distance in the middle of the road: cars on the descent would have more trouble evading him than would cars on the ascent, but he would take his chances. Derek was not fit enough to be a serious mountaineer. He set off, after assisting Den turn the car around and orient it backwards uphill. Gentleman, he laughed, start your engine, all three cylinders of it.

Reversing down a one way street always causes mayhem, even though the vehicle is going the same way as all the other vehicles. People find it disorienting. Reversing up a mountain pass, sometimes close to the white line in the middle, well, that gives other road users heart-burn. The ones going down the mountain had less time to make their views known, but whatever words they couldn't get out of the corners of their mouths they made up for by shaking their fists out of their window and holding their hands flat on the horn in the middle of their steering wheels. As if that was in any way helpful! On the other hand, I was an almost captive audience for cars making the ascent, which ascent we shared, albeit that they were driving forwards and I was driving backwards and rapidly getting a very stiff neck. They gave me heaps! I am glad I can't understand street French, German, Italian, Yugoslavian, maybe Russian for all I knew. I kept thinking to myself: Surely, it is not that hard to figure out that the person who reverses up a steep mountain pass must be in real trouble, especially when lead by a man dressed in a tartan blanket like a Peruvian taking his flutes for a walk. That held true until Derek had fallen behind by some distance, but, knowing Derek, still holding the shortest line between corners. But not a single soul offered to help. I have to say, after what we had experienced elsewhere, that one fact was a powerful shock. Not a soul offered to help. I inwardly converted every waved fist and every brandished finger into an accolade: just like the girls outside Halfords and the girls outside the pyramid, all these people knew, instantly, that I was Cliff Richard! All those fist wavers and finger brandishers, they were simply jealous, and that was sad. But, unaided, we made it. I went backwards into another "Stand here and admire the view" parking area. I didn't want to look: there are only so many views one can take in on any given day. I felt sick. Altitude sickness? Or the effects of a twisted neck making me feel nauseous? I didn't know, and what difference did it make anyway. At least forty five minutes later Derek appeared, the Peruvian pied-piper He was near frozen and gasping, his lungs fit to burst and every muscle and sinew in his legs probably about to snap as mine had been when carrying those two full waterbags. The one difference was that we hadn't set a time limit. I had left the engine running so that he would be able to thaw out quickly. And so it was that we proved to our limited satisfaction that, once in a mountainous while, we are forced to go backwards in order to go forwards, the most poignant of contradictions. And, in the words of Spike Milligan of the Goons, I had indeed been going 'backwards to Christmas'. Another year was closing out on us and we were not properly equipped. Life seemed to be leaving us out in the cold. (In 1980 Jona Lewie released the song called *Stop the Cavalry*, with the line "I wish I was at home for Christmas". A very catchy tune that became a classic. Every time I hear it, I am back there on that nameless peak in the Alps in early winter, waiting for Derek to appear.)

We took our time in the recovery space of our little home which was almost pleasantly warm. This was as much to let the engine and the gearbox cool down as anything else. And then I turned the car round and we sat and gazed. Facing the right way can be stabilising. We gazed. Wow! It really is a long long way down there and it is looking rather cold. The sun had dropped below the peaks and inside the car the temperature dropped in sympathy.

"Ah, well, Den. As you would say, let's look on the bright side. It's all downhill from here."

How far is downhill?

The ascent had been steep, very steep. The challenge thrown at us was the loss of 25% of the engine's power. The important thing on the ascent is power. The important thing on the descent is not so much power as the capacity to restrain power, which is to say, yes, brake power. We had driven across many thousands of kilometres and had only really had to use the brakes very seriously when driving headlong into a pile of tarmac and then driving headlong into debris from a landslide. Otherwise sand or mud or gentle braking had eased our cessation of forward movement. Looking down what seemed like a roller coaster ride into the bowels of the earth, or a world congress of hairpin bends, the issue of brake-power demanded attention.

"Do you think the brakes will handle this?"

"Only one way to find out, chum."

And down we went, like a ski-jumper onto the take off ramp. Predictably, the brakes overheated and went 'spongy', and several times on the downward spirals and switch backs we had to stop and let the brakes cool off, and then down some more, until we dropped into a breath-takingly beautiful valley, dotted with stunning chalets here and there looking almost perfectly peaceful. We arrived at the floor of the valley just as it was starting to get dark, and we knew we had to find somewhere to shelter because in the car we would freeze to death. The thought of crawling into our tent with just the 'tired' sleeping bags - not affording much protection - and the one blanket and our jeans on and shirt and t-shirt, that thought wasn't very inspiring. So I kept my eyes open knowing I had to pick out a likely 'saviour' as I had done in Benghazi. We passed one fairy-tale house with a barn beside it. I told Derek to stop. I walked over and knocked on the front door. After the experience of reversing up the Alps I wasn't feeling so optimistic. I knocked a few times more and stepped back a pace or two. The door opened, and there stood a very tanned, stocky man in his forties.

"Guten tag." That didn't sound so welcoming.

I repeated what he had said, and added a word of my own.

"Schlaffen?" I pointed towards the barn and, putting my hands together and resting my cheek against them, indicated that sleeping in a nice warm barn would be wonderful, didn't he think.

"Nein!" And the door slammed, abruptly. Slamming a door is like hanging up on someone. No "Aufwiedersehen". No "Schlaf gut". Just "Nein!" Slam. Silence.

I had always come up trumps, until now, and Derek probably assumed I would come back smiling. I didn't.

"We're stuffed. The bugger said no chance."

Rather troubled, we drove on until we found a partially sheltered area and pitched the tent. We had been through a lot together, and had only really had one tetchy moment, in Egypt, and that was remarkable given what we had been through. We had not pressed each other to speak or not to speak, to do this or do that, and everything we had done had been by willing agreement. And by now we knew each other fairly well without ever having gone digging for details. We knew where we stood with each other. And we both knew that this night was going to be a close call: we probably did not have enough clothing or bedding to survive the night. Neither of us felt comfortable about what we might have to do, but do it we would have to. So we go over our plan:

1. Get into sleeping bags, as close together as possible.
2. Spread the blanket over the top of us and tuck it in so it doesn't move during the night.
3. Stay as close together as two old badgers.
4. Pray we wake up in the morning and without ice on our eyebrows or frost bitten noses.

When we woke up it was still dark. We were stiff and felt cold in our bones. We looked around the inside of the tent by torch-light: there was frost all over it, and a thick frost at that - our breath was no longer really warm. Maybe it would be better if we got out and ran around or something, just to get our blood moving. I tried the tent zip: it had frozen solid and not just the zip; the whole tent flap was solid. It was thick with ice and refused to budge. My fingers went instantly numb and white and I gave up. We were trapped. And even if we could in fact easily get out if we had to - tearing through the tent - that wouldn't have helped because we would need the tent for a while yet and a tent with a large tear in it is useless in winter. We would just have to lie there and try to maintain some warmth, and wait for sunrise - if it was going to be a sunny day. The sun would melt the ice on the zip. We lay there for two or three hours until, mercifully, the sun did rise and slowly, but slowly, thawed out the zip. The very thought of being in the car again, after it had warmed up …. that wonderful prospect helped us imagine we were warm, but when we finally did emerge we were not warm at all and couldn't pack the tent up fast enough and get in the car and go, as far as we could as quickly as we could. We check our map and plot our route in principle and barring disaster: Salzburg, Munich and Stuttgart. The engine reduced to three-quarter power was a strange protection: given that the brakes were starting to give out, having to go slowly was advisable, and we didn't have a choice in the matter. Besides we didn't have enough money to have the brakes fixed; we barely had enough to pay for the ticket to tomorrow.

# CHAPTER 11:

# Breaking bread

With what very little cash we had left we would possibly make it to Stuttgart. After that we had very limited options: get paid casual work or starve or freeze to death. Winter was closing in and even the car heater was not coping very well in the fight against the cold. It is odd how things seem to accelerate the closer you get to a situation's unfolding. The bottom of the paper bag gets soggy slowly, but when the bottom gets too soggy, everything drops out of it very quickly. The seriousness of the situation was dawning on us at a rate of knots. Necessity is a hard task master as much as it is the mother of invention and we would soon, and very soon, have to become very innovative or have to choose between necessities: petrol for the car or food for us. Our diet was back to biscuits and water. We bought another packet of biscuits and pressed on, slowly.

The car continued to limp along as the roads got better and better and wider for longer periods and the rest of the travellers were going faster and faster. Except us. Even today I am amazed about how the engine of that car just kept going, against all the odds. I was amazed then that, just as the roads got better and wider, so we had to go slower. And all the while I had one other thought in my head: we have to find some paid casual work because we are on the brink here and make no mistake about it. It was winter, so we needed warmth and shelter and we couldn't afford either. We drove into the suburbs of Stuttgart and of course got lost. But what does it mean 'to be lost' when you have absolutely no idea where you are? We were not lost: we were finding our way. Yes, Den, look on the bright side. In Alexandria, Derek had become very agitated because we had become 'lost' and look what happened in Alexandria. Yes, we were finding our way, under pressure, yes, but finding our way. And in this state of finding our way, we passed a huge sign that read

## UNITED STATES OF AMERICA
## KELLEY BARRACKS

And the thought parachuted gently down onto the landing pad of my brain: Americans speak English; maybe we would get some paid work in there. I submit my brainwave to commanding officer Derek.

"Sounds good to me, son. What have we got to lose anyway!"

The strain was starting to tell its own story. His voice was downbeat. What we had to lose was something I didn't really want to think about, but it wasn't the car and it wasn't the clothes off our backs and it wasn't our shoes and socks and it wasn't dignity and it wasn't losing face.

The barracks were surrounded by a brick wall about five metres high, not quite high enough to stop a mature giraffe from peeking over the top but thick enough and high enough to keep the average intruder out. It had been built just before World War 2 when razor wire hadn't yet come into fashion in the world of high security. We reached the main entrance: the usual job, with large iron double gates, gatehouse, and the red and white pole that goes up, and two armed guards with helmets. We state our business, show our passports, sign the book, print our names, get our temporary pass listen to the instructions. The guard directs us to an office on the left further along the perimeter wall, near some workshops. The double iron gates had closed behind us, the red and white pole went up, and we went in. The red and white pole went down. We proceeded, without an armed escort, and without having had to answer questions about cameras and guns.

As casually as if we were leaning our bicycles against a shop, we parked the tired car alongside the wall, and went into the office. This was our first interview since Gibraltar. We showed our passes and asked the $64,000 question: Is there any work available? As it so happened, there was, for semi-skilled motor mechanics, taking care of oil changes, replacing filters, fitting brake shoes, tasks not totally outside the skills we had acquired in taking care of our mobile wardrobe. Derek and I looked at each other and agreed that, put the stress more on 'semi' than on 'skilled' and that's us to a T, innit. Plus, we had to add, we have had skilled experience soldering electronic circuit boards. We explained are qualifications. The word 'electronic' in the early 60s sounded very impressive so the fact that we had distinguished ourselves as modern young men set us apart from those who cleaned out toilets and dug graves or spent their free time at the labour exchange. Without further ado we were offered work and could start the following morning. Since we were evidently in transit, the guy who interviewed us let us know, it was understood that we would not be permanent employees, and that was fine because people were always coming and going and people were always needed there on the base. All we were asked was to do the job well and turn up on time. This was almost as smooth a transition as between Thompson and Debenhams and Halfords! Couldn't have been more straight forward. Naturally - civilisation is civilisation - we had to fill in forms. No big deal, as far as Kelley Barracks were concerned: paperwork made the world go round. Thereafter we were shown to what would be our home for a while: small room, but private - two single beds, sheets, blankets, hanging space, a couple of shelves. We didn't need more than that. Plus the radiators were warm.

That night we slept more soundly, and rather less coldly than the night before - we were not in the army now but we were 'in quarters'. We presented ourselves for duty at 8AM as advised. Stability has its charms. Warmth has a lot of charm. The workshop was well heated, and there was coffee on demand and food to be had at more regular intervals during the day than had been the case for most of a few thousand kilometres and several handfuls of countries. And Americans, as we knew from our 2.5 kg tin of corned beef, certainly knew how to eat well. During the day we were given to know that the US authorities were doing what was necessary to get us work permits from the German authorities. It sounded like a foregone conclusion. Not a job for life but wages that might at least help save our lives. (I still have the official typed letter offering that employment, in German.)

As to be expected, we first had to receive our 'kit' - overalls and working boots. Everyone needs a uniform sometime and we took our 'chits' to the stores to get fitted out. Perhaps because Americans know how to eat well, they are also taller than me. I was not in a tailor's shop, making my preferences known: I was in the world of 'standard issue' and was given my pair of overalls without even being measured. The legs were not quite twice as long as my legs, but it was after perhaps three or four steps into the legs of the overalls before they were anywhere near fully on - I finally had to roll them up at the bottoms. Overalls are slightly baggy anyway, but these were extra baggy on me, a situation Cliff Richard should not have to find himself in. We were then each detailed to work with a team, repairing lorries and jeeps. There is some protection in working in a team: you watch, pay close attention to what the other guy is doing and learn by copying, and fluff your way through if all else fails. After all, there are some key differences between the engine of a jeep or a lorry and the Ford Prefect or a Moto-Rumi scooter. The personnel had come from all over the place: Greeks, Germans, Tunisians, English, everyone earning the cash to convert into food and shelter, and fuel. We just needed enough fuel to get to Ostende, and further if we were lucky, and enough food to keep us awake at the wheel. But we were in no hurry. The workshop was cosy, and we were short on cosy, and the beds were comfortable and we had had enough of frozen zips in frozen tent flaps.

We worked hard and steadily, learning more and more by the hour. It was enjoyable. Come the 4PM hooter, it was down tools and off to the showers and changing rooms downstairs and then to the canteen for grub. Grub's good. Hot grub, even sheep's head soup and pig's trotters; that keeps you going and keeps you warm. Of course, having what is called appropriate clothing helps too, and a shirt and t-shirt didn't quite cut the mustard. We were back in the routine of working and everything went along smoothly, as it can, for two whole weeks. But then came the knock on the door. Well, this time it was the tap on the shoulder.

"Derek! Den! They want to see you in the office."

That day we had been working valuable overtime and the tap on the shoulder landed at around 7PM when it was already dark outside, and cold. It was explained to us that the application for our work-permits had been rejected. All very courteously explained. It was further explained to us that, since the work-permit applications had been rejected (Why? Had we been to too many countries?) we had no right to remain within the barracks and would have to get our belongings and leave immediately. All very courteously explained though we did not really understand the reason why we had been rejected. Our major concern was about the money we had earned but not seen anything of. And that concern was very courteously settled as well, and we were presented with our two weeks' wages and our payslips, crisp new notes and neatly typed pay slips with our names on. The one who delivers the shocking news can be courteous, and it's good that they are, but the receiver of the shock is shocked and being told to leave our patch of security immediately did not allow time to readjust, regroup, revise the plan that had assumed what was not to be assumed. We were, put bluntly, eased out on our ears and not so much as a gold watch from a Christmas cracker and a joke to groan over. Since Derek was expedition treasurer I passed over my thin bundle of Deutschmarks to him, he added his thin bundle and then stuffed our Fort Knox into his pocket.

Stunned, we wandered back to the workshop and down into the changing rooms to get back into civilian clothes again and then back to our quarters to pick up our wash things. There was a line of jackets hanging on their hooks on the changing room wall. I am thinking in emergency mode. The money we have is for survival between Stuttgart and England and fuel as well. Outside, beyond the cosy bosom of the workshop, even between the cosy bosom of the workshop and the white and red pole that is going to go up, it is freezing, literally. We were not appropriately dressed to contend with that. I eyed the jackets. Sometimes to survive you have to do the unthinkable: mum knew all about that.

"Degs."

He was dressed and ready to go, but he was sitting in a daze waiting for me to get those long overall trouser legs off and I didn't want to take them off. Even an undignified costume can be welcome protection. I spoke his name. He made a noise, that kind of absent minded noise that the speaker has to translate as "Yes, I am paying attention."

"Degs. The jackets. We don't have jackets. It's freezing out there."

He stared at me.

"And?"

"These guys will be able to get a replacement from the stores, no problems. They're military regulation issue off-duty jackets."

He didn't need convincing.

"We'll empty all the pockets and leave the stuff from each jacket on the bench below where the jacket was."

And we did that, each picking a jacket that looked like the best fit, very carefully putting everything neatly, including the wallets and cigarette packets, and small change and the ball point pen. It didn't feel good, but it felt a whole lot better than freezing to death. Having the jacket on I felt better already: it was a good fit. Between our quarters and the workshop and the car there was a row of trees, and all the autumn leaves crisp and uneven beneath them. We walked through the leaves and purposefully along the wall to the car. We drove slowly to the main gate, where the red and white pole went up and we signed the book, waited for the iron gates to slide open, and drove slowly out. At that moment it did occur to me that it wouldn't have been out of the question to have asked someone, during our two week tour of duty, whether we could not perhaps get our engine fixed. But it was too late now.

There are those ever so lovely moments that are so memorable. There are some clothes you have seen enough of and its time to dispose of them. You check through the pockets, just in case. Your hand feels something, paper, just a scrap of paper. But you take it out and, wonder of wonders, it's not a scrap of paper, it's a valuable piece of currency. Mercy be! What a turn up for the books!

And there are other moments, equally memorable but for exactly the opposite reasons.

We hadn't gone more than two hundred metres when Derek started tapping his jacket pockets. He pulled over, looking panicked. He was almost frantic.

"What's up?"

"The money. It's gone. I know you gave me yours and I know I put it in my pocket." He was now frantically going through all his pockets, muttering about what had he done and heaven knows we don't need this drama and so on and on. We got out and checked the floor of the car - back and front - under the seats, between the seats, between the seats and the doors. Nothing.

"I'm sorry, Den. I know I had it when we came out of the workshop."

"Well, we can't go back in because maybe the jackets...."

"We have to do something. We won't survive without it."

So we drove back past the main gate. We noticed that they were now locked anyway and the lights in the gatehouse were out. We parked a little further on than where we knew the office and the workshop were - we could just see the tops of the trees. We were desperate and desperate people do desperate things, and once again one of us had to do the unthinkable. One of us would have to break into a United States military barracks. Neither of us had had a whole lot of experience of doing that, but you live and learn. It has been well recorded in the annals of the English Educational system, Hertfordshire

Region, that one Denis Timothy Logan had excelled at gymnastics four years on the trot, indeed out-excelling everyone else. This skill had been acquired for very good reason. Well, two reasons. For one, it had enabled him to dance like Fred Astaire and do the twist in a manner guaranteed to make girls weak-kneed at the sparsely attended Friday night 'hops' as dance evenings à la rock 'n roll were called. And, crème de la crème, it had prepared him for clambering over fifteen foot walls. Derek Jakeman was more suited should a number of able bodied men be required to knock down a fifteen foot wall, but if that wall had to be topped, then Den Logan was your man. The threat of freezing to death focuses the mind wonderfully well. The thought of getting shot breaking into a military compound did not get a look-in.

"OK, Degs. Here's what's going to happen. You are going to stand close to the wall over there. I am going to climb onto your shoulders. With my arms stretched up I believe I will be able to get my fingers onto the top of the wall. Once I have got some kind of grip, you are going to put your hands under each of my feet and push me up a little so that I can heave myself over. I will then drop down and go about my business."

"Sounds good, Den, but the issue then is: How do you get back out?"

I have always been agile, nimble, float like a butterfly and stuff like that. I had springs in my feet. At school I would challenge the tallest boys: stand six or seven metres away from me, with your back to me, and don't bend your head down and I will leap frog over you with no trouble at all. And I did. Often. And the worst that ever happened was that I would lightly touch the top of a kid's head. I was a phenomenon, even outside the gymnasium and the dance-halls. And up onto Derek's shoulders I went, not much harder than stepping onto a ladder. He stood up straight, I grabbed the top of the wall (no broken glass up there either!), he pushed me up a ways and I swung over and dropped. Five metres is a long way down, but, as I said, I was a phenomenon. I just bounced on impact, sprang into an upright position and down to work.

We had walked through some of the leaves earlier, but in the dark and illegally inside a military compound one does not thrash about kicking leaves. I had to be stealthy and deliberate. I wasn't turning over one leaf at a time, but gently stirring the fruits of autumn with my foot, feeling for a lump that might be a wad of notes. The whole area was thick with leaves and covered a distance of perhaps thirty metres and three or four metres wide. Slowly, as quietly as I could I covered the ground, probing, bending down to feel with my hands only to find a thick twig or a lump of tarmac. No money. Start again. Derek does not try and communicate: he can hear me rustling around like a squirrel looking for nuts or a dog looking for a bone. Needle in a haystack? Worse: I am slowly going numb and the feeling is going from my feet. Before long I was going to lose the feeling in my fingers and that would make escape from Alcatraz almost impossible. I kept telling myself not to give up. I remembered how the sun had all but scorched the life out of Derek and I but it was that very same sun that was the primary agent in leading us back to our car and safety. I remembered being out of water, facing a gun barrel far too close to my nose. Don't give up; it has to be here somewhere. Start again.

After maybe an hour of this my brain was like cold stewed apple. It was of no further use as a brain. I have to trust my instincts because I have precious little else left. At a particular moment, my body just stopped moving: animals often freeze like that when danger is staring them in the face. I felt oddly calm. I looked at the ground, bent down, looked under a patch of leaves. Nothing. But my body refused to move away from that spot. I bent down again, and turned over the patch of leaves right beside my foot. I felt an edge, a straight edge. Think, Logan, think. I thought: leaves do not have straight edges. I took a handful of the leaves and whatever else it was: I peeled the leaves away and let them fall. My eyes must have been dancing like drops of water on a hotplate. I was staring at the envelope full of Deutschmarks. I could have wept. Instead, quite sincerely, I said, in a quiet whisper, "Thank you God, wherever you are." How these things happen, of course I cannot explain, but they had happened often, for us, ever since we had set out. I would love to have called out, "Degs! Degs! I found it! I found it!" but I did not fancy getting shot.

I picked out the tree closest to where I believed I had clambered over, put the money securely in the inside pocket of 'my' jacket, and rubbed my hands together to get some warmth into them. The tree was tall enough but there were no lower branches, so I had to have one leg against the wall and one leg against the trunk of the tree and inch my way up like that until I was into the branches. After that it was easy and I was sitting astride the wall. I gave a 'psst' to Derek who happened to be standing directly below, patient as ever. He had 'his' jacket done up to the neck and was hugging himself. I swung my other leg over as Derek got out of the way, dropped down, bounced and sprang back to my feet. Drum roll, applause, thank you thank you, and I gave the wad to Derek. He was impressed.

"How did you do it?"

"Heaven only knows."

It was a good job he didn't say, "What took you so long?" as I might have punched him, in good spirit of course. And that was our survival stash intact.

It must have been past 9PM and it was very very cold. After the evening's entertainment we were both stunned and got into the car and drove off without any idea where we were going to go. Our dear car was sounding laboured and moving in a rather three-legged kind of way. The Ford was now incapable of speeding. But we hadn't gone more than a mile when a blue glow drawing nigh changed the complexions of both of us - as if we weren't feeling blue enough already - and as if that wasn't enough, that blue glow was accompanied by the heart sinking sound of police sirens shattering the peace. For heaven's sake! What is it this time?! Why don't you just leave us alone!! But then I felt that wicked stab of guilt and the flush of shame: we were wearing stolen jackets, and how do we account for the wad of money!

"Degs. Do you still have the payslips?"

He felt in his jacket and took it out.

"Yes. Why?"

There wasn't time to answer as one police car had pulled in front of us and the second had pulled in behind and we're roadside again. Sirens off. Blue lights flashing, flicking colour around like a blue Catherine wheel. The usual instruction to get out. One policeman was checking the number plate. Ah. Foreign car.

"Where do you go?" asks the other.

"To Ostende," says Derek through a sigh that becomes a little puff of white air.

"Und where you stay?"

"We have a tent."

"Nein, nein. Das is not gut. Is late. You follow dis car. We take you to hostel. Ist free. Too cold for tent." He smiled. We smiled. They were looking after us. Why? We had been in many odd situations but for some reason this felt like the oddest yet, given our near-criminal circumstances. A procession of two police BMWs, engines as silky as a Swiss watch, blue lights rotating, and our precious little beige semi-invalid Ford Prefect sandwiched between them, cruising the streets of Stuttgart. Celebrities must feel good when worth a police escort. The two BMWs were probably worth more than Derek and I could earn in five years, but their purpose tonight was, for the moment anyway, completely for our benefit.

"You know, Degs. I could handle a chauffeur."

That sense of undeserved luxury did not last long. The leading BMW pulled into a courtyard and stopped in front of a heavy stone building with barred windows giving it the solid impression of being a prison. We left our dear beige mechanical friend to fend for itself overnight as we were escorted through a large, thick oak door and across to a reception kiosk also protected by sturdy iron bars. The two policemen explained our presence to the warden, wished us a good night's sleep, shook our hands and went back into the cold, cold Stuttgart night, probably sharing a quiet joke about the very odd things that young Englishmen seemed partial to doing and how good it felt to make sure no foreigners had a harder time in Stuttgart than was necessary. The irony of that situation was acute: the one time when police would have had good reason to arrest us (for theft of two jackets) was the very one time when the police were more concerned with our welfare than with any minor offences we may or may not have committed. Such is life.

Behind the bars of the kiosk there were two burly men, big fellows, about Derek's height but solid as rocks. We have to sign in after showing our passports and then one of the wardens leads us off to our quarters. It was every inch a prison and the walk down the bare stone corridor wasn't like the carpeted corridors of *Grand Hotel* at Benghazi or the passages in the Pyramid of Tutankhamen. We ended up entering our cell. Another 'first'. The eyes scoured the space: two bunks, a couple of folded blankets on each, toilet in the corner and metal sink in another. No crisply ironed sheets and no Chianti this time. The warden closed the door and vanished. There was a grill set in the door. We could hear quite a few drunks arguing with their disappointments. Through the grill in our cell door, we looked out and through the grill of the door opposite. In that cell was housed a guy with a bandage round his head. He gave us a friendly wave and put his light out.

And since there was nothing else to do, we settled down for the night as well, with our valuables (passports and money) in our money belts tucked under our pillows, and our second-hand jackets hung on hooks. We turned out our light as well, and that just left the sounds of the other blue chip residents groaning and grunting and perhaps fruitlessly demanding room-service or a better life. After a while I didn't hear anything which must have meant I had gone to sleep.

Institutions just love rousting people out of bed early in the morning, just in case the residents actually get enough beauty sleep to actually look beautiful in the morning. And that doesn't happen with a caressing, slightly husky whisper - Welcome to another day, darling. I do so hope you have slept well. Oh no. It's either a regimental announcement over a speaker right next to your ear and harsh enough to wake the dead, or, as in the case of this half-way house between the destitute and their destitution, it was the piercing shrill of a bell, like a security alarm or a fire-alarm sudden enough to cause panic or heart-failure. I woke up shocked: Hell's teeth, where am I? What did I do wrong to end up here? Did I kill Derek? No, he was over there, staring at me as if he has just been stabbed in the back.

"Morning Degs. Sleep well?"

"I did actually, until that cursed bell punctured my eardrum. How about you?"

"Not quite like home but better than becoming another item in the Bird's Eye range."

"It's lucky those coppers brought us in. Tell you what, Den, buy me a BMW and I'll be your chauffeur. How's that?"

And the events of last night trickled into the mind as we washed, sort of, in the small metal sink in the corner. And we sort of dressed, which meant that we put on our shoes and our second-hand jackets, and then we filed out as everyone else seemed to be doing. All the way along the roads we had travelled we had met an extraordinary array of ordinary people, each one of whom had made a contribution to our lives and keeping us alive. Each one of them had become important for me, and I am sure for Derek as well. I will perhaps never meet a single one of them again but I sincerely hope that, somehow, each one of them knows that my gratitude hasn't paled in almost half a century. Thank you, my friends, for without you I wouldn't be here writing this, and I am only sorry that it has taken me this long to say the thank you that you so deserve and many times over.

Everyone else had filed out of their cells and into a large room, a makeshift dining room. We joined our other overnight guests, perhaps forty unfortunates, young and old, down on their luck, close to wits' end, pulling themselves almost together to go out through that oak door and do whatever they could bring themselves to do. A big table offered mugs, fresh coffee and bread, at least something to break the fast since yesterday. We joined the queue, very conscious that the line between up and about and down and out is a very fine line that just about anyone can find themselves crossing at a moment's notice and not necessarily because of their own fault at all. And as we collected our mug of coffee and a couple of slices of bread I quietly acknowledged this strange camaraderie around me. After eating we joined the other queue shuffling along to sign out at the reception grill. Behind me was an apparition that I never will forget, the figure of some legendary soul, worldly wise and world-weary. He must have been over eighty years old. He wore a long and heavy army greatcoat and on his head a leather flying-cap with the earflaps and the strap under the chin that keeps the earflaps snug over the ears. (Seeing that cap brought back memories: his had zips on the earflaps too.) Covering that strap was a thick white beard. From one shoulder hung a large canvas bag and in his hand he held a violin case. We nodded to each other - he could easily have been old enough to be my grandfather or great grandfather even. He smiled. No doubt he was a repeat visitor, and perhaps this was what he accepted as his communal home.

He smiled again and slowly bent down and placed his violin case on the floor. I immediately thought, "Here we go. A solo section from *Swan Lake*." I watched discreetly as he opened up the violin case. Inside was a large lump of bread. Without a word and without looking at me, he took the large lump of bread in his two old hands. He stood up again, slowly as very old men do. Looking into my Lake District eyes from the bottom of the oceans in his eyes, he quietly broke the large lump of bread in half (much as mum had done when we lived on Blacksmiths Lane). He passed one half to me. I was back in the desert ready to die under the merciless sun, remembering my first communion. In a trance caused by such a simple but profound gesture of brotherhood, I accepted his gift and couldn't help bowing my head. I couldn't have held his gaze. Composing myself, I held his hand. He just smiled, a smile so full of understanding and compassion and patience that I have not yet fully taken it all in. We had a car, we had some money. We were still at the setting out stage, while he was waiting while there was time. He had given me half of the almost nothing he had to share. Derek was close to tears as well. As the line moved, we edged slowly towards the oak doors and reluctantly out into the steady drizzle of another day. Walking towards the car, I heard the words repeat in my head, *passeth all understanding*. In meeting that one old man I feel, even today, that I had met all mankind and shared half a lump of bread with all mankind. If I am ever hungry, I remember him. It is a great gift to be wise without speech.

Whenever Derek and I went through an experience that stretched one or both of us almost beyond our capacity, we would quite happily leave each other alone in silence as we separately and in our own ways allowed whatever the experience held for us to kind of wash over us and become absorbed. I had been fortunate with a travelling companion like that and I know that feeling was mutual. The car started - only once had it failed to start - but now it sounded like a broken motorised sofa. Not surprisingly we felt better for that good night's sleep, and rather meditative as well, while also feeling more secure with some money in our pockets and two second-hand army-issue jackets to keep us in the land of the living. We would feel better, though, when we saw Ostende and had bought our ferry tickets. We had drawn water from deep down in the well and there was no point pouring more water into a glass that was already full to the brim, if not overflowing. Half a lump of bread: what a gift.

# CHAPTER 12:

# All gone, job done

The car was chugging along at reduced power, 70 kms an hour if we were going downhill, but otherwise 60 kms an hour at best. There was no hurry. The countryside was beautiful, the roads were good and after crossing the Rhine we moved through Saarbrücken and into Luxembourg. The first night after Hotel Stuttgart was spent in the car, huddled up in sleeping bags, American army jackets and tossing a coin for the blanket. The next day took us around Bruges - the bypass saved us precious fuel - where fuelling the car and eating took us closer to the end of our salvaged booty of Deutschmarks, and we just took our time. After arriving at Ostende and paying for the ferry to Dover for us and the car, and buying another packet of biscuits, we had the equivalent of one English shilling left, and the needle of the petrol gauge was once again dropping towards 'E'. For the third time, we were setting out to sea. As when we were on the S.S. Ionia, we took along our own victuals, only this time that was not bread rolls but biscuits. For liquid sustenance we would use the same Coke bottle and top it up with water. We were tired but the crossing would be short and neither of us would need a cabin. We were enriched personally by what we had witnessed, and, quite frankly, we were worn out. The faithful LXD-521 was just about hanging in there. All we had to do now was get to that Clock Tower.

Derek and I definitely looked as if we had been across any number of deserts. On the ferry we looked at ourselves in the washroom mirrors and were mildly shocked: the contrast between us and the other passengers was very marked. For one thing we were basically dressed as if we were going on a summer holiday, while everyone else was dressed as if they were heading into Christmas. The guys' hair was stylishly done (or not) in the fashionable "D.A." - we looked like scarecrows. They wore clean drainpipe jeans. Our jeans looked like a fleet of trucks had driven over them. Our eyes did not look full of rollicking fun. Our skin was very brown. Other faces looked oddly pink. The girls looked good, and I couldn't see Sandrella anywhere. But all that stuff we had lost memory of confirmed that we were re-entering a world that we had forgotten we had left: it hadn't changed much, but we had. The smell of full-on English fish and chips and vinegar brought a smile to the nose.

I know it is a cliché, but when returning home after a long while, if Americans feel touched by the sight of the Statue of Liberty and French people feel touched by seeing the Eiffel Tower, it isn't surprising if English people feel touched by the sight of the white cliffs of Dover. We did, even a small lump in the throat. It was something of a blur after that, driving off the ferry and through Customs. Anything to declare? Are you kidding? We were pretty well cleaned out, and yet we felt full to bursting. We had to concentrate in a new way as well - back on the left side of the road. And we still had to get back up the A5.

On the outskirts of Dover the need for petrol was paramount and so we drove into what looked like a family owned garage. We had no money. Barter as a means of dealing with the transfer of goods and services was no longer current in England. A haircut and a few fags in exchange for a Burton's suit might be a done deal in Tunis, but Dover was not Tunis. I knew that because there weren't any goats or camels. On the other hand, we had no choice: one English shilling's worth of fuel would get us to the next roundabout if we were lucky, and we were going to need a good three quarters of a tank to get to that Clock Tower. On top of which we were hungry with a capital 'H'. Derek and I agreed that we would try and barter away the tent, sleeping bags, and Gaz cooker. The American jackets we would hang on to: we still had to keep warm.

"I'll stay here, Den. You seem to be good as this bartering bit."

I strode into the little garage shop. The bell did its ting-a-ling-a-ling thing and I stood by the counter. My eyes hadn't seen anything like this for what seemed like years: Cadbury's chocolate, Smith's crisps, Spangles, fags. I had almost forgotten why I was there when a man came in from the workshop, wearing a typically English flat cap.

"Yes, mate. What can I do for you?"

I had not felt at all embarrassed in Tunis bartering away my hire-purchase Burton's suit, but in Dover I did feel embarrassed explaining that we had crossed Africa and come all the way through Turkey and the Balkans and so on, and after all that and one thing and another the bare bones of our story was that we were broke. But, not entirely broke, I hastened to add - no one likes to barter with a completely asset-stripped beggar. We do have one or two fairly good condition items, I explained, on which we would be more than happy to favour you with the first right of refusal. The not altogether enlightened look on his face proposed that more specific detail was required. And so I pressed ahead.

"All we have got to our name are: one Bukta tent and two sleeping bags, on top of which we could possibly part with a Gaz camping cooker."

I would have understood perfectly well if he had scoffed and told me to piss off. Had we picked out a 'brand name' garage, one of those big name places, no doubt the franchisee would have tossed us out. But this was an ordinary family man proud of his independence, and perhaps something clicked because he thought for a few seconds, tapping his cheek.

"Hold on, mate. Let's backtrack a bit. Did you say you've been across North Africa, the Balkans, the Alps in that?" He pointed at our home on wheels.

"Yes."

"In that?" He laughed, incredulous, pointing again. "You couldn't cross North Africa in that! There's been a bloody war going on in Algeria for one thing. You must think I'm daft."

"Yes, we do know about Algeria. I think we got in at the tail end of trouble there. But look, here's the stamps in my passport. And I've got the Camping Carnet in the car as well."

"That's unbelievable. In that? Wait till I tell my missus."

He flicked through the pages of the passport.

"Lord above. Did you get to Tobruk?"

I nodded.

"My word. I was there in '43. Just imagine. You, in Tobruk, in a Ford Prefect. I had a tank and that was bad enough. You'd have only just been born then."

His smile was becoming more affectionate.

"Tell you what. Go bring in that tent and stuff of yours and I'll have a look at it. See what we can do."

I ran out, giving the ever-patient Derek a thumbs up, reached in over the passenger seat and got the tent and sleeping bags and Gaz cooker. Back in the garage I show him what he might be turning down if he said 'No'.

"Amazing." He kept saying 'amazing' as he turned over the sleeping bags, shook them, gave a quick eye-ball over the tent. "Amazing. Africa. Ford Prefect. Well I'll be."

He thought.

"Tell you what, son. Would six gallons get you back to.... where you headed?"

"Hertfordshire. St Albans."

"Right. Well, six gallons should just about do you. It's a deal. You happy with that?"

"Well, yes, but we are about as low on fuel as the car is, and if you could stretch your generosity to include one of those small Cadbury chocolate bars, well, that would be our dinner."

"Done." But he slipped me two chocolate bars and winked. Two? I questioned with a look. "One for your friend as well, mate. Though, maybe he only needs a half of one. You look like you need fattening up."

He filled up the tank with the bartered six gallons while he had a brief natter with Derek. And after that, we all shook hands - I could make a living shaking hands - and he waved us on our way. We limped towards London and limped through London. Derek kept forgetting that we were not in the same traffic environment as we had been since way back then whenever then was, and three or four times came perilously close to smashing the car. Around 4AM - our progress was painfully slow - it was all getting too risky; falling asleep at the wheel is as potentially lethal as falling asleep on a sand dune at noon. We knew a small 24 hour café outside Watford, *The Busy Bee*, and headed for that. We could wait there in the warm until after dawn and get back home around 8AM - not wanting to wake the family too early. Of course we wouldn't be able to buy anything but hopefully we'd be allowed to sit inside rather than catch a death of cold outside. Anyhow, fortune favours the brave, but maybe not the foolish.

There it was, *The Busy Bee,* all lit up all night long and condensation on the windows. Unbelievable. I thought about Wakeem and Salah and Dr. Anwar. What on earth would they make of a place like *The Busy Bee*? A transport café of that era was working class English to a fault. Grease, large mugs of tea, smell of eggs and bacon, stuff marked "Fresh" but which was anything but, Elvis on the jukebox, truck drivers' boots and a lot of conversation over the *Daily Mirror*. We went in, and the atmosphere hit us, not to mention the warmth. Derek went off to the loo. Almost immediately I felt this dig in my ribs.

"Denny Logan! What on earth you doing here, at this time of the morning?"

I turned on my heels.

"Dave! Good to see you too!"

"Didn't you do some mad-cap thing like drive to New Zealand? I'm sure I read that in the paper."

"That was the idea, but we never got to New Zealand. We did do Africa though. Just got back last night. I'll tell you about it one of these days."

"That'd be good, but I'm not at Halfords anymore. Got fed up. Happier driving a lorry. Better money, no one looking over your shoulder. Away from home most of the time. Anyhow, good to see you again. I'd better be off before the traffic starts building up. Catch you."

"Oh, Dave, just before you go. I don't like doing this but we're flat broke. Had to sell our tent and stuff to buy the petrol to get up from Dover. You wouldn't have a spare two bob would you?"

"Not a problem, mate. Welcome back." And he digs into his pocket and presses the coin into my hand as he says goodbye to everyone else. "See you all!"

And we bartered that coin for a coffee and a chocolate. Delicious.

Happily if briefly warm as toast, we headed off on the final stretch. And then it was the coasting slowly past the Clock Tower, along St Peters Street, down the hill past *The Ancient Britain* pub and into Francis Avenue. Timing is everything. It was knocking on 8AM and we had literally just put the handbrake on outside my home when, at that very moment, dad came down the path, flat cap on, cycle clips over his folded trouser turn-ups, pushing his bike. He caught sight of me, called out "Hello mate!" without a hint of surprise in his voice, threw his leg over the saddle, and rode off up the road. I wondered whether I had been somewhere else or not. I couldn't have imagined Africa, could I? Surely I had really been across the Alps, hadn't I? He hadn't even allowed me time to get my own "Hello" out of my mouth.

Before we set out, dad had bet me £5 I wouldn't make it. I never bothered to collect my winnings. I didn't need to, even though I was flat broke, skint, and pockets full of holes. Against the odds, we had made it! I'd lived with myself, cheek by jowl for months, faced death, broken bread with a destitute fellow traveller facing a bleaker and possibly shorter future than I did. But I hadn't come home: I was home, living in my own limited space, me, but a space that, in feeling, cannot have limits. I wore a wiser smile in love with what an open hand truly means. We hadn't taken a single photograph. We hadn't written a single word in a journal. We hadn't thrown a single punch. We had simply touched the world with our bare hands, and with our cheeks upon the pillow of the Saharan sand, upon which world are scorpions like spear throwers poised, and men in white suits; soldiers armed to kill and soldiers armed to protect two sleeping travellers. Contradictions everywhere and yet life is hugely wider than its contradictions. We had shared or sold everything we had, and, in kind, others had done the same for us. We had nothing left other than what we gave and what we had been given, and the jackets we had stolen - mine was my formal wear at my first job interview. We had absolutely nothing to show for it but we hadn't been robbed and we hadn't lost anything along the way. Well, no, that's not quite true: we had lost a door handle. But no scars, no scratches, no broken hearts, no broken bones, and no souvenirs to hand out. The most valuable souvenir was friendship and you cannot photograph friendship; you live it and share it. You may not be able to see it, but from time to time you do get to know it or hear about it or feel it touch you. And now at least you've heard about it, and read the proof. Life as it happened. And with that, I must leave you to your own journey across your own country and on that journey I wish you well. Go for it! God bless.

> Older Den: Now my job's done, isn't it, Den?
> Younger Den: Yes, Den, job done, and well done too.
> Older Den: You'll go far, young man.
> Younger Den: But after all that, we need a holiday, don't you think.
> Older Den: Yes. Where would you like to go?

Denis T. Logan
Caillou de Cogulot
24500 EYMET
FRANCE

Denlogan05@gmail.com